THE SEC

THE SECRET CYCLIST

Real Life In The Professional Peloton

YELLOW JERSEY PRESS

LONDON

5 7 9 10 8 6 4

Yellow Jersey Press, an imprint of Vintage
20 Vauxhall Bridge Road
London SW1V 2SA

Yellow Jersey Press is part of the Penguin Random House
group of companies whose addresses can be found at
global.penguinrandomhouse.com.

Copyright © The Secret Cyclist 2019

The Secret Cyclist has asserted his right to be identified as the
author of this Work in accordance with the Copyright,
Designs and Patents Act 1988

First published by Yellow Jersey Press in 2019

www.vintage-books.co.uk

A CIP catalogue record for this book is available from
the British Library

ISBN 9781787290211

Typeset in 11/15pt Fairfield LH
by Integra Software Services Pvt. Ltd, Pondicherry

Printed and bound in Great Britain by Clays Ltd, Elcograf S.p.A.

Penguin Random House is committed to a sustainable future for
our business, our readers and our planet. This book is made from
Forest Stewardship Council® certified paper.

CONTENTS

INTRODUCTION

I know that this book is going to spark a guessing game. Trying to identify me is going to be part of the fun, and I get that. As a reader, I'd want to know too. I'm not hiding my identity as a gimmick, though. I'm being mysterious because in my world riders are meant to be seen and not heard. I've been racing at the top level for various teams for around a decade now, but anyone who's spent even a short amount of time around professional cycling will know that offering an opinion in public is not the done thing if you value your contract. Even an off-the-cuff complaint about bar tape will get you in trouble with the team, because it's bound to get them in trouble with a sponsor. When I started out, it wasn't uncommon to see a team re-cover a saddle for a big-name rider who didn't like the sponsor's model just to keep everyone happy. They used to re-label tyres as well when they knew the ones they were supposed to use were no good. I'm sure they do it still. Our sport exists only because advertising and product promotion allows it to, so a rider giving his two cents about equipment is strictly prohibited. I know guys who've missed training rides because of dodgy groupset batteries and guys who have spent countless hours shivering and soaked through because their clothing sponsor couldn't make a decent jacket, but they're not allowed to tell you that. What domestiques say is just as – if not more – tightly controlled than their fitness and nutrition regimes.

I choose to be anonymous because while I want to show what professional cycling is like behind the ropes, I also have my career and my family to think about. Every public aspect of our lives is so tightly controlled that being truly honest is all but impossible in a newspaper interview, never mind a whole book. There are team guidelines for everything we do, and even something as innocent as borrowing the wrong kind of helmet for a mountain-bike ride with friends can land you in hot water if it ends up on social media.

Then there's the people. The race organisers, the agents, the other riders, the team bosses. Or, put another way: My colleagues, friends, employers. It has nothing to do with the *omertà* of the old days, it's just common sense. I couldn't show up to a training camp with all of my teammates knowing that I was going to write about everything they did and said, and I wouldn't expect my contract to be renewed if my manager knew I was likely to poke holes in his tactics publicly. If you don't believe me, I suggest you write a warts-and-all blog about your office, and put your name to it. Question how the business is run, make sure you remember to call your boss a moron, and then tell me how it goes.

It's a small world we live in generally, but the cycling world, well, that's just minuscule. Everyone knows everything, and no one forgets anything. When I set out to write this book, I didn't do it with the intention of offending anyone or settling grudges, but I didn't want to be excommunicated either. The truth can be hard to hear, and even when I'm only offering opinions, it would be impossible to share my honest thoughts on a lot of things if I knew my name was going to be plastered on the front cover. Cycling has been my life since I was a teenager, and despite all its flaws, I love it. It has been good to me, and I'm trying to be good to it, too. The purpose of this book is not to complain for the sake of complaining, or to slam anyone. I just want to show you what it's really like to be a professional cyclist, to give you an unfiltered view inside the peloton. There's a lot to like about the sport, but there are a lot of problems too, and I want to start a conversation about that. I've read books from the critics and the blindly faithful, and I never felt that I fit into either category. I've always thought that if you really love something, you have to see it for what it really is. To me, cycling can be glorious and it can be grubby, but quite often, it's neither. It's just pedalling for hours and hours for relatively little in return. It's fickle and occasionally foolish, but it's also engrossing and exciting, and most importantly, fun. With this book, I want to capture all of that.

GETTING STARTED

When I was little I saw the Tour de France on TV, and that had me hooked. I followed everything after that: the Grand Tours, the Classics, and the Worlds. I couldn't get enough of it. My dad had this collection of books about cycling, some of them were comic books, and that drew me in too, with all of the crazy stories and characters. The whole thing intrigued me. When I was eleven, I got my first bike, and I used to go bike-packing with my dad; even then we always did big days, so it was normal for me to ride a hundred kilometres.

I joined a club around that time too, but it was a little bit too structured for me at the time. I just loved my bike, so I did my own thing for a few years, and then went back when I was fifteen or sixteen. I was also busy playing football and trying new things, so cycling wasn't the only sport I was interested in. And I didn't come from a family with a big bike-racing tradition. We cycled a lot, but for pleasure.

At that age, football was easier, because most of the games were close to home and I could go by myself. Every so often, you'd have a big game far from home, but it was less complicated than cycling; you didn't have to drive for hours every weekend to compete. When I eventually started to race, I'd go with a friend of mine and his parents – my folks only started coming later when I got more serious. It's a big commitment for a parent, especially if you have other kids, because there's so much travel, so I didn't mind because I knew that my mum and dad had things to take care of at home. The more I got into it though, the more they became interested, and eventually my dad was driving me everywhere. It can't have been easy for him, but I think he liked it too. It felt like we were doing something important.

While I was in the junior ranks, I remember buying a new racing bike, and like a lot of riders I know, I promised myself that it would be the last one I ever bought. Talking to other pros, it seems to be a pact that we all make at one stage: you tell yourself that you're going to make it onto a team somewhere and be a professional rider, and get all the stuff for free. I wasn't ready for what was to come, but I wasn't giving up, either.

The training is one thing. If you love your sport and you're driven, it's not hard to get used to those demands. Your neighbours see you going out when it's lashing rain, or on a mountain bike when it's snowing, and they think you're crazy, but that's the job. I don't always like it, but I'd rather that than sitting in an office, and even when it looks shitty outside and I'm tired, I still love what I do. I've never hated riding my bike. I don't think anyone who's ever got a paycheque for anything can honestly say that they want to do it 100 per cent of the time, but that's why they pay you. For me, being a professional cyclist is as close as it gets to being paid to have fun.

There's no one 'right' way to train, either. It bugs me when people talk about training in a really dogmatic way, because we're all different. Everyone has to find what works for them, but incorporating something enjoyable into your routine will definitely keep you going longer. I've had a few teammates who never stopped for coffee when they were out training, for instance, but after riding with me they got into the habit. Those ten or fifteen minutes in the middle doesn't mean I'm lazy, it just means that I like espresso.

One of the riders on my old team never had sex before a race, and if it was a big one he'd go weeks without it. The first time I heard him say it, I laughed because I thought he was joking. That's some old-school nonsense, like he's Robert De Niro in *Raging Bull*. So the older guys all told him that it makes no difference, and he starting smiling and said, 'Oh! My girlfriend's going to be really happy. She's been pissed off with me because of this.' We were all laughing at him, asking: 'And what about you? You don't like it?' He just said, 'Sure, but it makes me tired.' Come on. There's no way you're going to have a long career or a happy home life if you're telling yourself that you can't have sex every time you want to perform well in a bike race. He's the same with food, so strict it's crazy. I've had a long career because I love riding my bike so much, but there's no way I'd still feel that way after fifteen years of denying myself all of life's pleasures.

On the opposite end of the scale, I used to have a teammate who loved ice cream and he used to eat it all the time. That's antithetical to what most riders are used to because it's so calorific, but he'd have two big ones on the rest day at a Grand Tour and then go out and finish on the podium of the next day's stage. A little treat can have a huge psychological effect. You'll still hear some guys say that that kind of thing is unprofessional, but how unprofessional can it be if he's able to go out and challenge for wins in the hardest races in the world? I love a beer, which some teams would definitely frown upon, but if I can't enjoy myself a little, I'm going to be in a rotten mood and it will affect my training. There are limits, obviously, it's not like a professional cyclist can consume a twelve-pack of beers and a box of cigarettes and expect to be in racing shape, but if you're out training for 150 or 200 kilometres almost every day, the odd gelato or a nice cocktail isn't going to do any harm.

What's really hard is leaving home all the time. Nothing prepares you for that. That's not just a cycling thing: ask anyone who travels a lot for their job and they'll tell you that it sucks. If you get to go on a trip every so often, it's fun, but it's a totally different experience when you're missing big events like birthdays and weddings. The shine wears off that apple pretty quickly. All of your friends and family are together, celebrating and having fun, and you're stuck in a mediocre hotel somewhere doing very little other than killing time in between training sessions.

A few years back, I was on holiday with my family and I was watching them, thinking that I wished I could do this every day for the rest of my life. I didn't want to think about leaving them, but I knew I'd have to. That feeling sucks. I'd probably only been home for a couple of weeks all summer in total, and before too long I'd be off again to a training camp or another race. When you have kids, everything changes so fast and you're not there to see it, or there to help, and it wears you down. Worse still, when I was home, I was tired and grumpy, and I would have been constantly hungry because I was trying to control my weight. My wife is my biggest supporter and she knows what it takes to do this, but I can't have been much fun to be around. That's depressing to think about when you love your family as much as I do.

That summer was a tough period, and I phoned my agent and told him I didn't want to do it any more. Obviously, he was a bit shocked and he tried to calm me down, but at the same time he knew where I was coming from. It's not an easy life at the best of times, and if you're unhappy you're never going to be able to be competitive. We worked together to come up with a plan that would get me back in the right frame of mind while still keeping the team happy, and that was a pivotal moment in my career. He knew I wouldn't budge once I'd made my mind up. That's the typical bike racer mentality. We're stubborn, and when we make a decision, we stick to it.

You have to or you'd be swept up by the broom wagon in every race. Even away from the racing, my house was the first one we saw properly with the estate agent. We'd looked at others online or in the brochure, but we visited this one, we liked it, so I bought it. Second-guessing isn't a good characteristic in this line of work.

My agent and I eventually settled on a good solution. I'd find a team with the right kind of atmosphere, where I could manage my racing days more carefully but still be ready for the biggest events. A guy like me, towards the end of his career, is expected to shepherd the team leader around the really big events, and in the right situation, make big moves in the mountains at a big race. Without wanting to be disrespectful to the smaller events, no one really cares if I'm at the UAE Tour or the Presidential Cycling Tour of Turkey. So that was the pitch from my agent: here's a guy who loves bike racing, has top-ten finishes at Grand Tours, does a serious amount of kilometres out training, but he wants to spend some time with his kids. It was probably not what they heard every day, but at least it was honest.

I can remember one team manager being a real dickhead. If the answer is yes or no, I don't mind, you have a team to run and I respect that, but there's a professional way to deal with it. Behind the scenes in cycling, a lot of the time it's more about macho bullshit than anything else. He told my agent: 'I want guys who want to race their bikes, not go on vacation.' Looking back, I think it's funny, because I've been a part of big wins, the kind of victories that his team couldn't even dream of. It's not the only reason that we win, but I think my current team is successful because no one in charge has a shitty attitude like that guy.

At the time, I knew I wanted to keep racing, but I also knew that I needed to find the right kind of team. Money was a secondary concern, because my rationale was that if I was happy, my career would last longer. I told myself that I didn't care about what other people thought, but looking back now, I did care a little. It's a weird feeling when you're in your early thirties and someone tells you that you're finished. In any other job, you'd just be getting started, but these managers were just dismissing me like I was yesterday's news. Coming back strong was a nice feeling. I don't like to carry grudges, but I think anyone in that situation would get at least a small amount of satisfaction from proving the doubters wrong. I'd be travelling somewhere beautiful, posting huge training rides on Strava, and thinking, 'You see? I can do it.'

Everyone could have told me to fuck off; in fairness, it's not like anyone wants to sign a rider who is asking for special treatment. We had a few meetings with different teams but I don't think the trust was there, it didn't feel like the right fit for either party. But with my current team, they saw my logic and they were willing to trust me, agreeing that whatever kept me the happiest was ultimately best for everyone. I'm not the kind of guy who goes partying or slacking off, so they believed that I'd be able to manage my own training once the conditions were right. The funny thing is that once I felt happy, I also felt like a better bike racer. I needed that time with my kids, without a doubt. Being a dad means more to me than being a bike racer. But the little bit of freedom also made me want to be a bigger part of the team, too. I raced less but I think I contributed more. Riding the bike was never the problem for me, but after so many years, the rest of it stank. Everything was about weight loss, travel, training – no family. The irony of it was that I'd have retired earlier if it wasn't for my team letting me off the leash a little. They let me do my own thing for a while and I came back as hungry as ever.

Without that change, I wouldn't be racing now. I used to think about retiring early, but only because of the travel and the stress. It was never the work. I think even when I retire, I'll still be out riding my bike all the time, trying to be fast and beat my friends. I love that part of it. I'm already a couple of years past the retirement age I used to have in my head, and now I wouldn't put a date on it.

I don't want to give the picture that I get special treatment or that I'm being lazy. During the busiest part of the season, I'm only home a few days a month, and less when there's a Grand Tour. The difference is that I get a good block of time after that, when I can be at home and hang out with my friends. It's crazy how important a dinner party and a few drinks can seem when you haven't seen anyone for ages. As for the kids, that time is worth all the money in the world. I was away for so much because it all happens so fast, but now I feel like I'm 'daddy', there's a proper bond and we have enough time to go have fun.

Starting out, it was all a big adventure. Imagine being a twenty-year-old kid being told that they'd get paid to hang out with their friends and travel the world. It sounds amazing. That changes with time, but the kid still comes out for things like the Giro d'Italia or the Tour de France. For the best stuff it's like being a junior again: I'll be excited about where the race is going, what the food will be like, what I'm going to see. Even talking shit with the boys and getting to spend time with them all, it's great. I'll be sad leaving home for a training camp in Tenerife or somewhere, but a big race? I still love it. That's a rare thing to cherish, and I want to enjoy every minute. Then, when I'm home, it's the same. The kids are growing up so fast and I want to be around and savour as much of it as possible. If the team can bag a win at a big event, that makes it all worthwhile. If it's a difficult season and you're at some shitty race, you question the decision to compete. But even then, I'll be analysing the tactics and enjoying my teammates because it's something that's in the blood.

Leaving a family at home is hard, but it also gives you something to look forward to. I pity the younger guys, stuck on their own in Lucca or Girona, coming back after a training ride to a lonely apartment and an empty fridge. The team camps must seem like great fun for them. When you're happy at home, though, no one wants to go to train at altitude and stay in some three-star hotel that's full of other cycling teams because it's boring and you'll probably come down in the morning to find that they've raided the breakfast buffet. It sounds like a joke, but if it opens at seven, there'll be a gang of hungry riders all jostling to get in because we're all starving. If I'm at home I have all my favourite food and it's not like I'm competing with my wife or my kids to get the good stuff before it's gone, so when you're away from home in January at the start of the season, looking at another year, it can seem like a crappy situation. I suppose pro cyclists get the January blues just like everyone else.

THEN AND NOW

When I started out, riders were generally home a lot more. Now, you're away for weeks at altitude-training camps before peak races, and you might only get to see your family for a couple of days in between the camp and the race. Back in the 2000s, I was on a smaller team and we definitely didn't have the budget for these long training trips, but I don't think even the top guys did much of that stuff – they probably just did a bit more EPO or some blood bags if they needed to prepare for something really big. Being able to do that makes a big difference!

Now you're either away training or away racing for most of the year. In the old days, riders got to spend a lot more time at home, even if it's true that they raced more than we usually do. For example, teams these days will begin preparing for the next season with a training camp in December and another in January, whereas when I began my career, riders were set free for the whole winter. If you didn't want to train, you didn't have to. The lazy ones could show up for the team presentation fat and totally out of shape, but now we have logs online with all our hours and power values for the sessions we've done, so even if we only take it easy for a day or two, team management know right away and you'll get a call asking what the hell is going on.

I can't say for sure exactly how it happened, but I heard a funny story from a few guys in the peloton last year about Zico Waeytens, the young Belgian rider. He felt that Team Sunweb had given him a really bad programme for the upcoming season, lots of small races that he didn't want to do, so to spite them, he went and booked himself an amazing trip to Tanzania without telling anyone. Of course, the team knew right away because he wasn't filling out the logs! It was not the smartest move on his part, obviously, because it was easy for them to figure out that he was up to something. And I can only imagine what his conversation with the team manager must have been like. At the end of 2017, he left the team by mutual consent, despite having a contract for 2018. I don't know if that attitude had anything to do with the move, but his new team, Vérandas Willems–Crelan, is Professional Continental, which is a big step down from the WorldTour and an outfit like Sunweb. Even the small events that a WorldTour team will do are bigger than the majority of races that will make up the Professional Continental calendar.

The balance of control has changed. Back in the day, you just rode your bike and did whatever you thought you needed to do to get yourself into shape. Now, the teams monitor everything and there's a lot less freedom. I don't want to make it sound like they're spying on us, but it's easy to see where a rider is just by checking the GPS files on Training Peaks, an app that we use to track our workouts. Maybe they'll have a look at your routes if your power values aren't improving or it looks like you're taking it too easy, and they'll certainly ask questions if you disappear to Africa on holiday. I really enjoyed Thomas Dekker's book *The Descent* for a variety of reasons, but perhaps the best part of it was when he reminisced about how insane the cycling world used to be a decade ago. I like to enjoy myself when I can, but no professional athlete should be living a life that involves clandestine meetings, bags full of cash, or high-speed crashes. He was an extreme case, but in a lot of ways he was also the epitome of cycling in that era, and for all his personal flaws, the sport has a lot to answer for because it should have taken better care of these vulnerable young guys and made sure that they weren't being led astray.

If I'm slow to criticise the cheaters too harshly, it's for that reason. It's terrible that people were able to so brazenly abuse the system all those years and I have a lot of sympathy for the guys who feel like their careers were short-changed, but at the same time, they didn't come into the sport as bright-eyed kids dreaming of steroids, Erythropoietin, or blood transfusions. That change only happened when they were absorbed into dirty teams and exposed to dodgy teammates. I knew Thomas a little bit when he was still riding, and I think he'd have been wild whatever he did in life, but it was crazy for me to think about some kid flying around the world, partying and meeting doping doctors, and no one had a clue.

I don't think cycling – or any professional sport – is 100 per cent clean today, but there's no way anything like that could happen now. We used to be expected to show up to the race in good shape and that was it, whatever else we did was our own business. We're less independent now, and it makes it more like a proper job. I don't mean to say that it used to be easy, because that's one word you could never use to describe professional cycling, but sometimes it feels now like I have office hours. We used to be more like cowboys. And there's certainly more paperwork. I think careers are getting shorter as a result. It's probably partly due to the workload, but also due to the stress. I don't think you can hold yourself together these days for ten or twelve years at the very top of the sport. I see it with teammates, constantly worrying about contracts and the future, and you can actually feel it in the bunch, especially in early spring, because there's so much on the line. Cycling has become more scientific in terms of training and tracking a rider's performance, and because of that, it's also become more ruthless. Results are everything.

When I first turned pro, the level of the bunch was like a pyramid. The best guys did everything right – and a lot of them did everything wrong, too, in terms of performance enhancements – and the rest of the peloton just rode their bikes a lot, and then went to the races and rode themselves into shape. Now, we all have power meters, coaches, target values, dietitians. And not just the top guys. Most teams will have five or six coaches for around twenty riders. On my first pro team it was one guy for all of us, and he'd just make one training schedule that was very short and easy to understand: 'Do this all winter, and we'll see you in January.' It's raised everyone's level, even the domestiques. The watts I'm pushing now, for example, used to be good enough for a top-ten finish at almost any race, guaranteed. Now, it's thirty or forty guys on the same watts. It's easy to think, 'Fuck, am I bad?' and get depressed about it, but it's actually not that at all, it's just that everyone else has gotten better.

The improvements in terms of professionalism have been crazy to see. I miss some things about the old days, like drinking a beer with the guys before a race, but everyone has improved so much and we're all really focused on diet and fitness. Sometimes I'll go out to dinner with my wife and, while I'd order some fish and a salad, maybe a small glass of white wine, she'd go for a burger or a steak with a beer. Obviously, when the waiter comes, they always get the orders mixed up and I'm sure we look funny swapping plates and drinks. That's the job, though. I'd love to stuff my face with chips and lots of fried stuff, but I'm being paid to stay skinny and to make sure I'm ready to race. You see a lot of the rookies struggling with that at the beginning. They'll try to do things that normal people do, or kick up a fuss when they have to eat a massive bowl of plain pasta after a stage, but they get no sympathy from me, because that's what we're being paid to do.

Another big change is that hardly anyone drinks any more. The pro tour used to be wild, but now we have to live like monks. The teams have stepped it up too. These days every rider gets treated so well, they have nutritionists, they work closely with coaches on personal programmes, they study their power values – it wasn't so long ago that only riders like Lance Armstrong could train like that. Spending time in the wind tunnel was unheard of not long ago, unless you were a big time-trial champion like Bradley Wiggins or Tony Martin, but now everyone does it. You even hear amateurs talking about their VO2 max tests, it's crazy. If we're picturing the professional peloton's talent levels as a pyramid, it used to be really steep, with a huge gap between the top guys and the rest of the bunch, but now the bottom of the triangle is really wide. The best still rise to the top, but everyone just below them is on a similar level. That's made it a lot harder for the support riders. If you were a domestique ten years ago, your job was to work for the first 150 kilometres of a stage, and once you had done that, no one really cared if you had a beer in the evening or didn't watch your diet. Domestiques can't do that any more – if you give anything less than 100 per cent all season you'll be left in the dust.

I was one of the first riders to get a power meter. I bought it with my own money, and even when there was a blizzard outside, I'd go out on a mountain bike and do a few hours. That was my advantage – a willingness to go the extra mile. But now, the advantage that serious approach to training gave me has been diminished because everyone is on top of their weight and their training all year, and everyone dedicates a lot of time and money to camps so that they can fine-tune their condition together as a unit. That's not such a big investment for the richest teams like BMC, Sky or indeed Inios for that matter, but for the rest of the peloton it's a significant portion of the budget. And it's not just the top guys, like back in the day. I remember going to Tenerife one winter because I wanted to ride a really strong Giro d'Italia, and I paid for it all out of my own pocket. Now when I go, some of the hotel car parks look like they do during a race, full of team cars and mechanics' trucks, and out on the ride I'll see Vincenzo Nibali with his whole Bahrain–Merida team preparing for the Giro or the Tour. A medium-sized team like Cannondale or LottoNL–Jumbo might only send five or six guys at any one time, but that's still a lot of money, maybe €20,000 for the group for a couple of weeks. The hotels are fully booked in April, and the team managers will already be planning the next season's camp a year in advance. They'll even organise camps during the Tour de France for the guys who aren't racing. I remember not so long ago that if you didn't get called up for the Tour squad, you booked yourself a nice holiday on the Mediterranean and enjoyed the sunshine for a while before restarting the season with a few days' training hard in the mountains near home. That's a huge change in less than ten years.

The biggest teams have their own personal chefs at all the training camps and the races, and some of them even have their own dedicated kitchen trucks, but even the little ones will employ someone that deals with nutrition and rider diet. You used to just eat whatever soggy pasta the crappy hotel restaurant was serving, and at home guys could be drinking beer and eating chips. Look at how skinny everyone is. I used to be one of the leanest, but now I'm average. You can't even have a snack without someone having an opinion about it. I had a huge argument a while ago with my team because sometimes I like a chocolate bar instead of an energy gel when I'm racing. The nutritionist didn't want to sign off on spending team money on junk food, and I'm a grown man screaming, 'Just give me the fucking Snickers' like a child.

It's a different sport in a lot of ways. Look at the sprinters: everything is designed specifically for those few seconds before the line. Special bike frames, helmets, skin suits. It's incredible. I was always against that stuff because it felt a little bit like a gimmick and if I'm honest, I like the romantic idea of being a bit old-school, like I'm too cool to wear my aero helmet. But I've started to, because you can't afford to ignore the advantages. David Zabriskie is the first guy I remember wearing all that stuff for a road stage, and it looked so silly to me. Like a lot of guys I laughed and thought he was crazy. But it turns out he was just ahead of the game.

How we train is totally different as well. These days, racing days are more or less limited to around eighty per year, but when I was younger, it could be as many as 110 or 120, because I did a lot of small races and criteriums. The modern season is more about blocks – blocks of training and then blocks of racing – but back then, I was pretty much going from race to race, and when I was home I wasn't training hard, I was just maintaining the level and recovering, so I only had to ride for a couple of hours a day. The racing days have been cut down, but with all the camps and altitude training, it's more days away from home. If you're a GC contender now, you'll be away from home at altitude for a couple of weeks before a big goal. That's hard for me, because I didn't become a professional cyclist to train, I wanted to be a racer.

Sometimes I wonder about how many days I do at the 'office' every year, including travel, training, and racing. I'm certain that it's more than a normal job, and the travel means that most of the time, even when I'm not doing the actual work, I'm still away from home in a hotel somewhere. During the season, I'll take a day off every two weeks. That's the only day I don't ride at all. But that's not a real day off: there'll be team emails to respond to, maybe another bike fitting, or a visit to a masseuse or a chiropractor. Also, it's not like we all have pro mechanics living with us when we're home, so the bike needs to be cleaned and maintained and that takes time too. I think that normal people would call that a working day. I love it when I reply to an email from one of my sponsors or a business partner on a Saturday night, and I get a reply on Sunday. To me, that's a good worker, because that's what my life is like. I can't understand out-of-office messages, I'm not that kind of person. Some people I do business with only work four days a week. It must be nice for them, but I can't even imagine it. It's partly my mentality, I know that, but it's also a requirement of the job. Pro cyclists are always hustling. We have a small window in which to make money, and it's not like we're earning the kind of salaries that footballers or tennis players get, so we have to supplement our earnings with side projects. I looked up the PGA Tour's earnings list recently and everyone in the top-100 had made more than a million dollars this year. That kind of money would make you a team leader at a lot of cycling teams, but there are some golfers who've never even won a tournament on the PGA Tour and they're multi-millionaires. We don't have that luxury, so the smart guys in the bunch are all studying something or starting businesses in their spare time so that they'll have something to fall back on once their racing days are over.

We used to always have a local training group, six or seven guys from different teams who live nearby. It was a good way to stay in shape in the off-season because we could push one another, and it was a bit of fun, too. I loved the communal aspect, going out for a few hours' training and then stopping for some coffee or a bit of lunch. Now everyone has their own personalised programme, so it's impossible. There's a gang of guys in Girona that have a big group ride, but they only stick together for an hour and then everyone splits off to do their own thing. The social side of it is totally gone. The younger guys seem to distrust that kind of training, preferring to just go solo and do whatever the coach has scheduled for them on the computer, but if you look at the data, I don't think you lose anything by hanging out with your friends as long as you're all serious about training. And I know I'd rather race my friend up a mountain and have some fun than just do structured stuff alone while staring at a little screen. With my friends, 'interval' is a dirty word. We just go fast. That's the training programme. It's not so empirical, but it keeps it interesting, and ultimately that's what will keep a guy in the best shape possible. There's no way you can have a long career if you don't enjoy riding your bike.

The first rule of cycling is that you need to suffer, and no one else can do that for me, and no computer or programme from a coach is going to make it hurt any less. It seems like a lot of people these days start with the last 5 per cent, the things that sound impressive, like the personal trainer, the intervals, the wattage targets. But none of that is going to win you races if you can't sort out the first 95 per cent, and that's all up to you. When I'm at home, I have my gym, my rollers, my turbo, I like to use Zwift sometimes, I have a guy who'll drive the scooter for me when I'm out riding. The improvements that the teams have made over the course of my career have been incredible, but ultimately, I'm a professional athlete and it's my responsibility to take care of myself. As my coach used to tell me, 'Cycling is a tough sport, but it's also boring.' If you want to be good, you have to ride your bike every day for five or six hours. You'll go home, have lunch, take a nap, maybe go for a walk, then dinner, and sleep. That's it, over and over again.

If you're not in this game, that can be hard to understand. We're not out doing hour-long cafe rides or skipping days because of the weather. In the space of a month, a pro might do as many kilometres as a keen amateur would do in a year. I love that cycling has opened up a lot in recent years, and embraced a wider audience and new technology, but it's annoying when people who don't understand the sport comment on what we do, or when the data is misused to make a point. Guys will look at the power values in the middle of a flat stage of the Tour, for example, and then come on Twitter to tell you that they could do that. OK, they could hang for an hour or two in the middle, but there's no way they could handle the final kilometres because the pace is crazy, and we're doing that repeatedly for three weeks. It's not always meant in a mean way, but it can feel a bit disrespectful when you see that kind of thing on social media, because I've poured my whole life into this, and I don't want to see somebody just playing the pro to look cool on Instagram.

The old guys found a way to balance the drudgery of training and the hard labour with some company and some laughs, and that's what kept them going. I try to explain that to my younger teammates, but it's hard for them to understand. I'm still a young man in the grand scheme of things, but for some of the kids coming into cycling I probably sound like a pensioner.

I used to watch my more experienced teammates and then try to do the same. That's how I learned to be a pro. When I joined my first big team, I remember noticing right away lots of little things, like the fact that the best riders, a group of Spanish guys, never took the stairs, only the elevator, even for one floor. They'd never eat dessert, at the most they'd have some fruit and a bit of yoghurt. I'd come from a team where I was used to eating some pie after my dinner, and one of the sponsors was a beer company, so we always had a pint or two, but all of a sudden I was surrounded by these guys who paid attention to the smallest little things. That was hard, my first season, because I was on the minimum wage, and when we were in one of the nicest hotels I've ever seen for the Tour of Qatar, I took advantage and ate everything they put out, all these amazing cakes and sweets. Then I saw how much faster those Spanish guys were going uphill, and the penny dropped. They were humble and very serious about their work, it was just train, rest, and eat well. That's the base to a good career, regardless of whatever pharmaceutical help they had afterwards.

For that reason, I don't like when clean riders blame all their woes on doping. The dope definitely played a big part back in those days, but as a young rider coming into that world, I saw a huge difference in how riders approached the sport. A lot of people were taking the piss, drinking and smoking and not really taking care of themselves in the off-season. If you had enough talent, you could do that, and just about get by. But the best riders were always the ones who worked the hardest. Maybe they were all taking something too, but part of the reason they were dropping me on the climbs at the beginning was because they took better care of themselves than I did. That was obvious to me, and it was something I could fix. I knew from an early age that I wasn't willing to cross the line when it came to drugs, but I could narrow that gap by training harder and eating right.

Thomas Dekker, for example, was so talented. More than me, with or without the drugs. It's true that he also had a talent for dope – his body responded really well to it. Even away from racing, I remember him talking about some party he'd been to and mentioning that he'd been up for days on ecstasy. But that guy put the work in, even as a kid. As a junior, he'd do 180-kilometre training rides when the races were only 120 kilometres. It's the same with some other high profile riders who have had run-ins with the authorities or even served bans; you can't just put their success down to doping or disregard what they achieved because of their chequered pasts. You can take all the drugs in the world, but you're not winning the races that these guys won without an enormous amount of talent and an even greater amount of hard work.

It's easy for people on social media to speculate about these guys or call everything into question, but talk to the majority of riders in the peloton and there's a lot of respect there, even from the most ardent anti-dopers, because we see the work ethic up close. It's also worth saying that Valverde has always contested the ban and doesn't speak about the ruling. Although I never did drugs, doping had an impact on my career, and when I look at my results, it's impossible not to wonder what I could have achieved in a cleaner peloton like the one we have today, but at the same time, it's not like all they did was take drugs and then become world-beaters. Valverde is old-school, he's constantly riding his bike, no intervals or anything tailored like that, just plenty of hours in the saddle. The year he was suspended, he did something like 40,000 kilometres. Every morning you could find him at this meeting point at a roundabout just outside Murcia, waiting for his posse. He always trains with a big group of friends, guys he likes to race and have fun with.

One year we were training in the Sierra Nevada mountain range in Andalucía, and he was there with his team too. As we got ready to go on a ride, a group of guys showed up at 9 a.m. just to hang out with him. It was a two-hour drive from Murcia. We were in different teams but in a situation like that, it's nice to go out as one big group, and he took charge. The plan was to ride for a couple of hours as a bunch, stop for some coffee, and then go hard. Some of the other guys on my team were getting a bit angry about it because they thought it would be slow with all these amateurs, but honestly, after the coffee stop it was insane, those guys were flying, launching attack after attack. I don't think I've ever gone that hard on a training ride.

We ran into him again a few days later, and after a while a couple of the Spanish pros that were with us started teasing him, saying, 'Hey Champ, come on, do some work on the front.' Valverde said he didn't want to because he was saving himself for a good time on the climb, but they kept it up, joking with him, 'Come on, you can do a bit of work and still do a good time, you're a champion.' So he starts riding hard, and as we got closer to the main climb of the day, the pace was really high. He was chatting to everyone, he took some phone calls, and near the top he glanced over at one of the other guy's computers to see what his heart rate was. Then he started to laugh. 'Hey man, you're already at 170? I thought you wanted me to go hard!' A kilometre or so from the top we were all begging with him to slow down but he just kept laughing, saying it was our fault for putting him on the front. In the end, I escaped because my trainer, who was waiting after the summit, saw us sprinting around the bend and just started screaming to slow down. Later that evening in the hotel, we found out why Valverde was so happy to race full gas – he'd planned to take the next day off! That kind of thing makes me smile. He lives for cycling, and that's why so many fans and riders still love him. Watching him at the 2018 World Championships in Innsbruck, it was impossible not to smile. The Worlds had always been the 'one that got away' for him, despite his incredible success almost everywhere else. He won two silvers and four bronzes over the years, which is a feat in itself, but at thirty-eight, most of us thought his chance at gold had passed. In the final kilometres, though, you saw he was a real champion. He looked comfortable on the final climb, while Romain Bardet and Michael Woods looked scared of him. He was the best sprinter in that trio, so they didn't want to do any work for him. Being made to ride in front like that would have unsettled a lesser rider, but even as Tom Dumoulin got close to their group, he didn't panic. He did look a little bit shocked when he finally crossed the line though, and I thought his emotional response to the win was infectious. I know a lot of fans will refuse to be happy for him because of the doping ban he served. But I don't think we can be as black and white as that. There are a lot of people involved in professional sports that have a murky past, but once they've been punished, we need to believe that both they and the environment can change. Otherwise, what's the point? Do I believe that riders like Valverde can serve a ban (which he has always refuted) and then come back to competition and win without scrutiny? I don't know, but I'd like to think that I've seen some riders who have definitely doped change for real. There's no way to say for sure. I will say something that I think is important: I believe that some guys are just more talented than others, and we shouldn't forget that. Valverde races a lot, he loves to train, he takes great care of his physical condition, and he's always at altitude. Those things count for a lot. After the suspension, he won the hardest stage of that year's Tour Down Under – his first race back. Then he went on to take stages at Paris–Nice and at the Tour, came second at the Vuelta a España and got bronze at the Worlds in Limburg. He hasn't stopped since then, either; he has almost 100 wins in his career and the majority of them have come since his comeback. And the Movistar team have shown a lot of trust in him, because they certainly don't hand out three-year contracts to many thirty-eight-year-olds.

I don't like to dwell on that period too much because it would be easy to get depressed about it, but at the time when the worst stuff was going on, I was in a different league. I never saw the stars like Jan Ullrich or Lance Armstrong, apart from some meaningless criterium like the Profronde van

Stiphout, after the Tour de France. I knew them from TV, but while they did the Monuments and the Grand Tours, I was racing at the Tour of Belgium or the Flèche du Sud in Luxemburg or the Tour of Austria. There were other, lesser-known dopers there too, for sure, but I never felt like people like Armstrong robbed me of anything. I preferred to focus on the positives, and I felt so lucky, this young guy getting to ride his bike for a living, make some decent money, and see the world. All I wanted to do was be a pro, and if I was lucky, save some money to travel with my family when I retired.

It's a shame that more of the dopers from my generation haven't opened up about what really happened because I think that there are still some doctors and managers involved in the sport who have a lot of questions to answer. I remember that in 2010 the French newspaper *L'Équipe* leaked the UCI's list of suspicious riders for the 2010 Tour de France, a list that ranked everyone from zero to ten depending on how dirty they thought the riders were. Given the fact that Armstrong was only given a four, it's fair to say that there was a lot of bullshit involved, but there were only two guys, Carlos Barredo and Yaroslav Popovych, who were ranked at ten, and they both strongly disputed they were ever involved in any doping activity.

Nowadays, I look at riders like Esteban Chaves, Bob Jungels, Julian Alaphilippe, or Tom Dumoulin, and I see a totally different kind of cycling. I definitely think that guys like that can win races in the right way. If Dumoulin starts beating Chaves up 18 per cent climbs, or Chaves starts winning long and flat time trials, I might change my mind, but the new generation is more believable. And even when it was really bad, I don't believe that absolutely everyone was dirty. For one, I know I wasn't. And I could list some old teammates that I'd be willing to vouch for. I've finished in the top ten at Grand Tours, and for my talent, that was a huge achievement. Can I believe that in those years there were a handful of guys at the races who were better than me, without any performance-enhancing drugs? Sure I can. Out of the current crop, almost all of the best riders have shown a clear progression since the junior ranks.

Perhaps my biggest concern about the young riders is how far they're willing to go to lose weight. When I joined the pros, everyone was lean, but they weren't skinny by today's standards. They hadn't a gram of excess fat on them, but they looked healthy. That really changed around the time of Bradley Wiggins. Lance Armstrong was never less than 73 or 74 kilograms, which is heavy enough for a cyclist of his height, but he kept it at that level because he didn't want to give up too much power or run the risk of illness. Look at the guys today, and he seems huge, because Chris Froome is ten centimetres taller than him but he weighs five kilos less. Standing beside Romain Bardet and Rafał Majka is almost scary, but they go uphill seriously fast.

It seems like some riders are pushing the weight too much. I think Tejay van Garderen has come out and said that about himself. He's a tall guy, so trying to get below 70 kilograms is going to be difficult, and it has consequences too. You'll get sick, and bones break easier. Last year at the Tour, Froome blamed his collapse on the stage to Col de Peyra Taillade, when he lost twenty seconds in 200 metres, to the fact that he hadn't eaten enough on the previous flat stage. So you can push it too much. I've struggled to find the balance over the years and I've been guilty of going to extremes as well, but I worry that the younger generation are going to really go overboard. I'm already certain that cycling has a major issue with eating disorders. At an early season race, a GC rider might be at around 7 per cent body fat, but that drops right down to around 4 per cent for a Grand Tour. To put that in context, a healthy number for an adult male is around 14–17 per cent. Getting down to Grand Tour weight means pushing the limits of what's possible for a body, and it also means walking a knife edge between being light enough to win and not so light that you're going to get sick. Being skinny as hell is great on a sunny day climbing in the Alps, but if you get one rainy day (or some snow at the Giro) you risk losing it all because your body is too weak to fight off the cold.

It's a subjective thing, but it also seems to me to be under-mining the real appeal of the sport. Guys lose a lot of weight and get really good at staring at their power meters, and then they complain when the course at the Tour or the Giro is too technical. Cycling is an exciting, and sometimes dangerous, sport. There's no getting away from that. I've been in a lot of crashes over the last fifteen years, so no one feels for someone more when there's a bad wreck at a race, but I don't understand riders when they come out to the press complaining about the course and demanding change. Like Richie Porte at the Tour in 2017, when he crashed out on Stage 9 on the final descent after the Mont du Chat climb. He was pushing his limits, and obviously he went too far. It happens. Guys like Peter Sagan and Vincenzo Nibali are incredible on roads like that, because they're naturally talented bike handlers and because I bet they train hard on technical terrain. That's an important skill for a professional bike racer to have, and a big reason why fans around the world tune in to watch races. It shouldn't be taken away just because some guys can't stay upright. No one forces us to go that fast, you do it because you want to win, and to win, you need to take risks. That was a tough break for Richie, he looked to be in good shape and was aiming for at least a podium, but it was worse for Dan Martin. The Irishman was going fine until Porte took him out. He lost time and after the race, tests showed that he had broken vertebrae, and it could have been a lot worse. There's no alternative, though. Riders like Porte can be as fast uphill as they want, but if they can't handle tricky little roads, fast descents, and difficult surfaces like gravel or cobbles, you don't deserve to win a Grand Tour. We're not racing on Strava, or on exercise bikes in the gym. Cycling is supposed to be hardcore.

THE SEASON

I'm going to try to sum up a typical season, month by month. As far as I'm concerned, October is the end and the beginning of every year. I know that they've changed the calendar in recent years and some big races like Il Lombardia are now later, but I'm usually fucked by then. I can't race any more. As for races like the Tour of Turkey or the Tour of Guangxi, I won't even look at the results. If the team decides to send you, there's not much you can do about it, but in the bunch you'll hear guys joking about licking tables and drinking out of every water faucet they can find, just to try and get sick. Whether they actually do it or not, I don't know, but it gives you an idea about how most of the peloton feels about these events. It used to be a month off. You'd finish the World Championships and then take some time for yourself, hang out with friends, maybe a little vacation with the family. The younger guys go away with their girlfriends on fancy trips, but it's not as easy once you have kids because they're in school. I'll still ride a couple of times a week with friends, but it's relaxed.

November is one of my favourite months. We'll start training again, but locally, I'll just go out with some other pros that I'm friends with and we'll have a good time. At that stage, it's just important to get back into the swing of things, you don't have to worry too much about weight or power values. It's like going back in time a little bit, to before I was a pro, just riding for the fun of it. Whatever you do is good: if it's four hours, great, but if it's only two, you don't need to stress about it. If you live somewhere with a lot of pros around, it's the time of year when you'll see them all together, regardless of teams. If you're in Monaco, you might find Chris Froome out with twenty guys, just enjoying themselves.

Up until recently, December was a free month too. There were no team camps or anything like that. You might get together with some other guys and rent a villa somewhere warm, but that's about as organised as it got. People came and went as it suited them, it could be five or six guys from different teams, hanging out together in Spain for a couple of weeks. That was really nice. I never had a problem motivating myself for training, so I could get some good work done in an easy atmosphere. But now, most teams start the camps in December. It's still fun, but it's work. There are meetings every night, coaches and managers are there watching everything, maybe some new sponsors or technical partners that need to be introduced. And for the older guys like me, some boring meetings that we've done a hundred times, about the log books or whatever. And by then, the Tour Down Under is already looming. The guys who are going to that will be really focused, they won't eat too much or drink a beer over Christmas, so even if that's not on your calendar, the stress from that creeps into your life a little bit. It's the only time of the year that the whole team can be together. Basically, before you've had a chance to really unwind, the circus is up and running again.

The season proper starts with a red-eye flight to the annual team launch. There isn't the time, or, to be honest, the budget, to make those journeys in a leisurely manner, so usually I leave my house as early as possible in the morning, get to the hotel and do some gym work before a team meeting and then, more often than not, a dinner with the sponsors. It's taxing. The day after, there's the big event with all the media followed by a long press conference, and then we'll go straight to the airport, for another flight to the training camp, before ending up in another hotel. You could be anywhere. The next morning, our schedule begins, so that first night you'll sleep like a baby. It's three days of hard training, followed by a rest day, and three more days of riding before we head home. If you're looking at someone's social media, it can look like we're living the dream, getting to jet off to sunny locations in the middle of winter, but the reality is far less exciting. Don't get me wrong, the warm weather is a nice treat, but the rest of it is pretty boring – it's just train, eat, sleep, repeat. Most of the time I don't even get to the beach. The rides usually start a little later so it's not so cold up the mountain, which means you're leaving at around ten and you're back to the hotel around 4.30 or 5 p.m. Then it's a late lunch, massages, some stretching, a meeting about how the camp is going and what's coming up the next day, and then it's dinner time.

All that said, when you've got a young family at home, training camps can seem like a nice break. It's a good time to get some business done, too, so while I'm writing this, I'm also catching up on emails and considering some offers. I don't mean that in a bad way, you miss your kids, but I don't get woken up at 6.30 a.m. here and that's a luxury I rarely get at home.

It's around this time of year that we also have a team meeting with the sponsors. There'll be some time to hang out and have a big dinner, and it's usually pretty relaxed, especially if it's been a good year, but it's important for the sponsors because it's the only time that most of them will get access to the riders. For the stars, that could mean that they're totally booked up all day with photoshoots. Over the course of a pro's career, you'll be asked to pose for some weird stuff. My fellow riders and I have posed with everything from kitchen utensils and barbecues to mattresses. If you want to know what it feels like to be a professional cyclist, get into your full kit and try to keep a straight face while someone photographs you bouncing around on a bed. Tacky cycling advertising is something of an art form. It's not as bad as it used to be – cycling is trying to modernise and be a little more stylish – but there are still some great examples out there. Hansgrohe, a company that makes bathroom and kitchen fittings, ran a campaign recently with a half-naked Peter Sagan in the shower – with his bike, for some reason. And not too long ago, Sidi had Vincenzo Nibali and Ivan Basso dressed up as chefs with a shoe on a silver platter. I think the tagline was 'The winning recipe'. They also did something with a totally nude Filippo Pozzato, covering his shame with, you guessed it, a pair of Sidis. Cipollini Bikes had Mario Cipollini evading capture in a ridiculous James Bond spoof, but he's the boss there, so he brought that one on himself. During the Tour one year, I was flicking through the channels and I came across Tommy Voeckler getting chased around a velodrome by some rugby players. I still have no idea why. I suppose the sponsor stuff is fun, in an odd way, and that's what pays the bills.

I look forward to the first training camp every year. It's nice to start with a clean slate and to look forward to new goals, and it usually renews my enthusiasm for bike racing. That week also includes your twenty-minute test, which sets your benchmark levels for the year. Some guys get nervous about it, because it will show the team where you are in terms of condition, but as I've gotten older, I worry about it less. Even if you're not in good shape, it's a useful wake-up call, while there's still enough time to do something about it. The younger guys will be more stressed about that because they could go up or down, but at my age, I more or less know my level and I know that it's not going to change much. When I was younger, I stressed about it too, I wanted to show how good I was, but nowadays I'm looking at the bigger picture. If you know you're

a bit heavy or you're lacking power, with six or eight weeks to
go before you start racing, you can catch up. Some years, your
season is practically over after the Tour, so it's a pretty big gap.
It's not like you're suddenly five kilos overweight, but it can
creep up. The testing provides some focus, and usually I know
myself how I'm going anyway, so if all you need to do is keep
a close eye on your diet, it's a bit of motivation – watch your
weight, and you'll be fine.

I've never minded the long training sessions, I love riding
my bike. And even though there's not a lot of down time, you
can work in your own routines, there's time to do some core
work or some weights, because unlike the races when there'll
be sponsors and media, you don't have any other engagements
or any transfers between stages to deal with. We try to get a
bit of socialising done as well, like a nice dinner out on the
town. The hotels are a lot better than they used to be, but
you're not getting a beautifully flame-grilled steak at the three-
star buffet, so it's good to get out as a group to talk and share
some personal time.

Getting the new clothing is always a trip. There's so much
of it, but to spoil the prestige a little bit, you usually have to
pick it up off some guy with a truck on the motorway nowhere
near your home. When I was a neo-pro, I think I had four bib
shorts for the whole season, and now we get twenty. It's a lot,
but not as outrageous as it sounds, because with the kilometres
we do annually, stuff wears out. Every year, I'm doing what
the average club rider does in four or five years, and I have to
do it no matter what the weather, so the kit can start to look
grubby quickly, which is a no-no for the sponsors, and there's
always a few crashes. At the beginning of my career, all the
gear made me really happy, and you can see how much the
younger guys on the team enjoy it, there is so much of it. After
a certain stage in your life though, it becomes more of a chore

than anything else, because you have to spend the whole day at home clearing out closets and drawers, and figuring out what you're going to do with the old stuff so that you don't get caught out riding with something like last season's shoe covers. It's stupid, but a sponsor will get really mad about little things like that so you don't want any of the wrong kit hanging about the house. A lot of it can be given to friends or kids you know locally, but there's not a lot you can do with five team-branded skin suits. I have a really big fan who has tried to buy some of it from me in the past, but it's not worth the hassle. I make enough money, and it's nice to pass it on to people who appreciate it. A lot of it actually goes to a mechanic at my local bike shop, so in return I know I can always call for a favour, and all of my friends wear the same sizes as me, so they're well dressed, too. It's not like that for everyone, though. At the end of the year, there's always a joke of a race in Japan, le Tour de France Saitama Criterium. If you ask me, ASO are just taking the piss out of the riders to make some money at the end of the season. But all the big stars will be there, and definitely the jersey winners from that summer's Tour. It's hard for me to understand why someone like Chris Froome would go there, because he already makes millions every year, but he always shows up. A few years ago, they did a photoshoot with him in a sumo wrestling suit. Anyway, last year, some friends of mine saw him running around wearing nothing but his bibs – he had literally sold the shirt off his back. I know that some riders go over with a suitcase full of the old clothing, and sell it to the fans there. I understand a guy who's on a small contract, but a rider at the very top of the sport?

The team will take new bikes to the winter training camps, and at the end of that the riders will take those bikes home with them to train with. So if you've ever seen a pro out riding in the winter on last year's bike when his team has changed sponsor, it's just because he hasn't gotten his new bike at the camp yet. There's a lot of logistics involved with supplying a team, and it takes time to get all of the new equipment to each rider. In the old days, everyone would fly in, maybe with a bike, and the mechanics and soigneurs would drive the team cars, but I guess it's cheaper to do it this way now. I'm not sure if most fans realise it, but even at the big teams, expenses are controlled to the cent, so there would be someone complaining about costs if I was carrying my bike bag with me on Ryanair all the time.

In my early years, my team never even did a December camp; I used to organise one myself with a few of the guys I was friendly with. We'd rent a house, plan some routes, and just take care of ourselves. Planning wasn't very scientific; we'd go out on the balcony in the morning, look at the weather, lick a finger, stick it in the air, and make a call about which direction we wanted to go. There was more opportunity to let your hair down back then. Now, even if you're all together in the centre of a city for a sponsor event or the team presentation, no one wants to go out. That's better than everyone, full of testosterone, getting drunk and heading to a brothel, but it wouldn't be so bad if we all went out for a beer or two together. We could still be in bed by twelve, feeling like we'd done something that young people do, that friends, and normal colleagues, do. Years ago, I think I drank twelve bottles of Tripel the night before the presentation because I was pissed off about my schedule, and a teammate came with me to drown my sorrows, but things like that seldom happen now. Today's cycling is too micro-managed and serious for that.

In January, Down Under used to be a cool race, by which I mean not stressful. You could go there in January, enjoy the nice weather, do some training beforehand, and the race was big but not as important as it is these days for the teams. Now you've also got the Cadel Evans Great Ocean Road Race before it, so it's longer away from home. The teams go earlier too, to avoid jet lag and to get used to the climate, so it's like a mini campaign right at the beginning of the year. You might be gone for thirty days – and who wants to be gone for a whole month so early in the year when you already know that you'll be gone a lot during the spring and for the Grand Tours? I know some guys go to China in October and then Down Under in January, and in between, they'd have a team training camp. So they couldn't really even take November off because they can't afford to lose too much form.

In my head, February is still when the proper racing starts. There are races like the Volta ao Algarve and the Ruta del Sol, which might not seem like big races to casual fans, but they're really stressful for the young guys because it's there that they realise the size of the step up from the lower ranks to racing with the big boys. It's not that the veterans don't get a bit nervous, but after doing it ten times, you're not going to worry too much.

I just enjoy it now. I love being away with the boys, that's the life of a professional cyclist to me. There's no way I'd have survived in the peloton for so long if I didn't enjoy that aspect of it. Being with the other riders, joking around with the mechanics and the soigneurs, that still puts a smile on my face. I hope that doesn't go away. I know that the guys my age enjoy the camaraderie and a lot of us will go out of our way to pick up some beers for the mechanics and go over for a chat, but I see a lot of younger riders closing themselves off, spending a lot of time on their own, watching Netflix or scrolling through social media. It's a change of the times in general, I suppose.

I really like this time of year, but it's better to be in Europe for it. That's the real cycling. I'd rather go to a shitty little race in the middle of nowhere in France than fly out to Dubai or Abu Dhabi. Those races look more glamorous, but I've never really cared about that flashy stuff. The only thing that I know I'm missing out on is the food – the pasta in France is terrible. And the hotels ... Let's just say that France has a lot of catching up to do. They can be grim. I've slept on a fold-out bed so many times. You're a professional athlete, and they put you on a fold-out bed. It's crazy. And the rooms are so small, especially for two guys with all our kit. Imagine the smell of it all after a long rainy stage, with the dirty shoes drying out by the radiator and there's no room to move because there are suitcases on the desk, under the beds, whenever we can fit them. The only other things in the room will be a couple of cookies and a kettle with some sachets of Nescafé. You wouldn't wish it on your worst enemy. None of the staff at those hotels give a shit, it's not their own, they don't care if a World Champion or a Grand Tour winner is staying there. In Italy, it's different. They're usually run by families and they love having the riders there. It's something that they take pride in.

On the plus side though, for the rest of the year, I can look back at those horrible plates of soggy spaghetti covered in thin, bland tomato sauce, and count my blessings because whatever is on the menu, I know it will be better than the stale buffets at the Classic Sud-Ardèche or La Drôme Classic.

It's also great to see those places in winter. You get one picture when you come with the Tour de France, but it's summer then, hot and sunny, with thousands of people on the roadside. It's a completely different place in February, all the colour of summertime is gone, it's cold, and it can feel empty. I like to enjoy those differences, and it's nice to be able to walk into a cafe and sit down with a coffee or a pastis without all the crowds. We have more time to ourselves at this point in the season, and no one is going to say anything if a couple of guys go out for a beer before dinner. There's no way we could do that at the Giro or the Tour. Those little races in France, Spain, and Portugal are still important, I don't want to make it sound like no one cares about them, but they're not going to be a major goal for a WorldTour team and so at that point in the season, everyone is just trying to stay relaxed and ease into the calendar. Logistically, they're also easy to manage, because they're limited to one area. There are no big transfers or anything like that, so we have time to hang out and they only last for five days, so everyone's full of energy. At the Giro, I'll still have energy at the end of the first week, but I don't want to use any more than I have to because I know I still have two weeks to go.

At the end of February and the beginning of March, all eyes are on Belgium. There's still a month to go until the really huge events, but all of the big Classics riders want to lay down a marker early on and if the team has a Belgian or a Dutch connection, there's huge pressure to win. Omloop Het Nieuwsblad always kicks off the Belgian campaign, and if you look at the winners' list, it shows you how much an early win means. When I was young, it was guys like Peter Van Petegem and Johan Museeuw winning every year, and since then it's been dominated by real champions like Philippe Gilbert and Greg Van Avermaet. I used to love watching those races when I was a kid. Museeuw was awesome.

For a lot of the Grand Tour riders, March also means Paris–Nice. It's a shit race, through no fault of the organisers. There's so much stress in the bunch because everyone is fresh and looking for an early result. Getting a win or finishing high up on the general classification so soon in the year will take a lot of pressure off a rider for the upcoming season, and after a winter of training, everyone comes into it thinking that they're the new Eddy Merckx. It takes a few months for them to realise that they're still the same guy they were back in October – it's not like Santa Claus came over the winter and transformed them into champions. Everyone thinks they can win every bunch sprint, every mountain stage, and all of that means lots of crashing, lots of nervous tension in the peloton. And the weather doesn't make it easy; they call it the 'Race to the sun', but the weather usually sucks. Tirreno Adriatico is on at the same time and if it was my choice, I'd always do that instead. Racing in Italy is always fun: good food, nice coffee, and the fans are always brilliant.

One of my worst days on the bike was at Paris–Nice. It was a very long stage, with shitty weather, and we got dropped badly in the final move so we ended up twenty minutes or so behind the leaders, riding into a rotten head wind. At the finish, the team told me that the hotel was around four or five kilometres away and that it would be quicker for me to go by bike, because there was still a lot of race traffic. That was fair enough, but all they told me was that it was a Mercure hotel. I started following the Mercure signs, but when I arrived to what I thought was my destination, there was another team there, not mine. One of their mechanics told me that there were two Mercure hotels in that city, and that my team were in the other one, five kilometres away. I got there in the dark, soaking wet, it was early March so it was cold too, and after six or seven hours on my bike I was totally fucked and out for blood. I was furious with the soigneur who'd just sent me off without any directions, but then I saw that there was food waiting for me, and I completely forgot what I was mad about.

The Volta a Catalunya is different. I like that race. It's the oldest in Spain, and it's unpredictable, because they always plan these mountain stages without knowing whether or not the roads will be passable. I like that they keep trying. It's all in one region too, so it's usually pretty easy getting to and from the hotels, and the fans are great. The best fans though, they're at País Vasco, the Tour of the Basque Country. They know every rider's name. It's not like Ventoux at the Tour de France when most of the fans are tourists who only know the main stars. In the Basque Country, they know us all, they know the races you've won, they cheer for everyone. Up in the mountains, the roads are so crowded, but in a good way, it's a festival atmosphere. You can usually smell a lot of weed in the air. They're out to have a good time and enjoy the racing. The food around San Sebastián is incredible as well. It's a shame, actually, because up until a few years ago, the teams would only bring a chef to the Grand Tours, meaning we were free to eat the local cuisine. That might have been a negative racing in France in February, but it was a big plus when we got to País Vasco.

It used to be that País Vasco was the big one, and Catalunya was more for the neo-pros and the smaller teams, but these days Catalunya is raced at a really high level, all the big guys are there as part of their preparation for the Giro d'Italia. In the last ten years or so, I've seen a big change there. I think that changing its position on the calendar helped a lot. It used to be in mid-May, so it clashed with the Giro, but since they moved it to March it's perfectly timed for the guys going to the Giro, and for the riders who are aiming for the Ardennes Classics in April.

Back in Belgium, the Classics are in full swing by early April. Races like Paris–Roubaix and the Ronde van Vlaanderen are where my heart is as a fan, but as a rider, I was never built to win them. When I was a kid, those were the two races that I'd never miss. I'd be glued to the television. I might watch a replay of Liège–Bastogne–Liège, but I'd never miss Roubaix or Flanders. Flanders is the home of cycling. The history in Italy and France is very rich too, but it's more spread out around the country. In Flanders, it's all condensed, crammed into this little corner of northern Europe. The crowds are incredible, and the emotions of riding those roads are like nothing else. The first time I did it, I was so proud. Ask any rider who's done it and they'll tell you that it's one of the most incredible sensations you can have in your career. I preferred the old route to the new one, but when I think of all the money that those VIP stands on the Kwaremont must make, I can understand the decision. And it's great for the fans to be able to see the racing more than once during the day. That's something that the sport is missing. I love the tradition of waiting on the mountainside for a Grand Tour to pass by, but you only get a few seconds of the action and it's hard to understand what's going on at that point. That will always appeal to the hardcore fans, but it's difficult to explain to an outsider.

Milano–Sanremo is earlier, of course, but it's great as well. It's not a race that suits me and I've only done it a few times, but you can feel the history there. It's more interesting than a lot of people think, too. You hear people calling it a flat race, but there's no way you can win in Sanremo unless you can get over the climbs. I think that's what pissed off so many people in 2016, when Arnaud Démare won. He's this big sprinter, and yet he had the fastest time on the Cipressa climb, faster than guys like Michał Kwiatkowski, who are really good uphill. I didn't see what really happened, but a few senior riders accused Démare of holding on to the car. There was no photography or video proof to back up the allegation so it didn't get taken any further, but it did come up again during the 2018 Tour de France. The Sanremo route really gets interesting after the tunnel at the top of the Passo del Turchino, descending down into Liguria towards the coast, where it rolls along until reaching the final lumpy climbs where something always happens. It might seem boring at times, but it's a really tactical race and while you wouldn't design something like it if you were starting a new race today, there's so much history attached to it that you couldn't change it, either. I was really happy to see Vincenzo Nibali win in 2018. He's attacked in the finale of Sanremo a few times but never got it to stick, and I love seeing the big general classification riders giving it a go in one of the one-day Monuments. It's old-school, you don't often see it any more. Anyway, there's nothing else like the Monuments, and no amount of Hammer Series events or new races in Asia will change that. Maybe the next generation of fans just want two solid hours of spectacle, they don't have the patience for old sports like cycling, but then it's better to go watch the X Games or something. I've tried to figure out what the Hammer Series is a few times, but it just made my head hurt.

The Tour riders can have a little break in April, but obviously if you're doing the Giro too, it's a different story. It's time to say goodbye to your girlfriend or your wife, because you won't be seeing much of them for the next few months. There'll be altitude camps, preparation races, and a lot of travel. One year after the Tour, I counted backwards, and out of the hundred days before the finish on the Champs-Élysées, I was only home for nine or ten. It was all altitude, racing, altitude, racing. For example, the Tour de Romandie is always good preparation for the Giro, but in between you're lucky if you get home for a couple of days. It's a great race though, I don't think there's a stage race on the WorldTour that gives you more time to rest, because the stages are short and there are no transfers. The only bad points are that the weather isn't usually great, and the Swiss can be real dickheads. They'll charge you if you want an extra pillow in your room – they charge you for everything. Not that the riders are picking up the tab, but I know I wouldn't go there on vacation. Go up to Lake Maggiore, and on the Swiss side, a plate of pasta is

€25. On the Italian side, it's €8. A steak could cost you €50. Normally during a race, the teams aren't allowed to put anything on the tables, because the hotels need to make some money. But in Switzerland, the organisers allow them to bring their own water to dinner, because a bottle from the hotel would be seven or eight euros. With seven thirsty riders and all the staff, that really adds up. It's a beautiful place, though, and they know how to organise a good race. The Tour de Suisse is always enjoyable. They even charge the teams to hook up the electricity to the trucks. I suppose that in the old days, they had liquid altitude. There's no need to spend two weeks on top of a mountain if you're pumped full of EPO. Mentally, it's become a lot more demanding because of that.

I'm always torn about May. The Giro d'Italia is special, there's so much history and it's always beautiful, but I love the Tour of California too. It's 'foreign', if that makes sense. In the cycling mentality, everything is in Europe, and the races all matter so much. When we're in the States, the teams are more relaxed, thanks in large part to the American temperament. Everything is possible, everyone wants to give the best service possible, and they're definitely not charging you for extra pillows. The teams rent big RVs, there's lots of space for us all, and in the hotels we all get queen-size beds. You'd never get that in Europe. Most of the time there we're crammed in like sardines in some crappy chain hotel. The attitude of the people makes a big difference, and over there it can feel a bit like a holiday. The American people are more chilled out. If you're racing in Italy, for example, they're all really frantic, probably from too much espresso, they talk a mile a minute and they can get really worked up about things. There's more of an easy vibe in California. It's a big race, but not so big that it will make or break a season. If we can get a good result, it's a big boost, but if it doesn't go our way, it won't ruin the whole summer. You see a lot of teams hanging out in the evenings at the hotel, eating outside, maybe doing a barbecue, it's a brilliant atmosphere. And everyone loves Mexican food, which is obviously great on the West Coast. The coffee is shit, but you can't have it all.

If you already know that you'll be on the Tour de France team, June is pretty easy. Otherwise, you're going to be a ball of stress, trying to convince the directors to take you. Every day is important. Some younger riders or domestiques might not know for sure until after the Tour de Suisse, which is only a couple of weeks before the start in France. The team will tell them: 'If you want to come to the Tour, show me something.' The pressure is incredible. Even though most of the media and the fans will only concentrate on the leaders and the big names, the Tour de France will change a career. Even if you're just going to ferry water bottles up from the team car, it's the highest level you can get to in our sport and everyone wants to say that they've done it. It's something to point to, to be proud of. Even if you're talking to someone who has no idea about cycling, they'll know the Tour.

Normally, the team will have five or six guys who will definitely go, and the other two or three spots are up for grabs, and seven or eight riders will be competing for them. I loved my first Tour, making the team was a great feeling, but I was still young enough that it wasn't make or break. I knew that if I didn't get called up then, there'd be other opportunities. I did OK, but it was still a dirty time in cycling and it was really hard for a clean rider to compete. I'm not saying it was impossible because I still think that talent counted for a lot, but you only have to look at the big names from the mid-2000s to know what I mean. Not many of them were free from controversy. People were still getting popped regularly for CERA – the third generation of erythropoietin – and blood doping.

The stress of the Tour doesn't only affect the riders, either. You see it across the whole team, from the mechanics and the soigneurs right up to the directors and the managers. It's the race of the year in a lot of ways, everything leads up to and depends on a good July, and everyone wants to be perfect. There's no margin for error, and you're always under scrutiny. Even down to silly things, like if a rider asks for the salt and pepper at the dinner table, you'll see a couple of them jump right up trying to be the first one to pass it. It's counter-productive, in my opinion. Stress never helps anyone, and they'd be better at their jobs if they just treated it like the other races and relaxed a little. They're the same as the riders in that way: you don't make it onto the Tour team as a mechanic or a soigneur unless you're the best, so if they just work like they usually do they'll be fine. It's impossible for a rider to live in a bubble at a big race, we're all in close quarters, and we spend almost every minute of the day together as a team, so one person's stress can infect the whole group.

In the bunch, there are always a lot of crashes in the first week. There's less space between the riders, we all want to get as tight as possible, everyone's terrified about being dropped or being left in a bad position, and the turns are just that much quicker, the braking just a little bit later than usual. You can feel the tension. It's changing, though, and not in a good way. When I started, it was only the Tour that felt like that. Now, most WorldTour races are charged with this nervous energy. People ride Catalunya like their lives depend on it, and maybe they do. Their livelihood, at least. There's always pressure to perform, all year. It used to be that at the preparation races, the teams would be spread out around the bunch, guys would go to the back to chat to their friends, but now it's always a rehearsal for the Tour, even in February or March you're trying to show that you're together as a team and that you're always working hard for the leader. Teammates might even bicker about their position on the road, because guys want to be up towards the front pulling or right behind the guy who's pulling, because they're more visible that way. It's bullshit. In theory, it's better to be close because you can react quicker, but cycling is a tactical sport and you know the places on the course where something could happen. It's important to be together around the leader when you know the move is coming, but the rest of it is just for show. It makes for a lot of stress and not much else.

Come August, you might be finished with the Tour, but you're not finished racing. The criteriums come thick and fast, and it's always a crazy couple of weeks. It's probably why I've never really gone wild partying in Paris. Some riders like to, but I know what's coming so I have to stay focused. I'm also dying to get home at that stage. After the Champs-Élysées, there'll be a reception for the team and by the time we eat dinner, it could be eleven o'clock and then I'm ready for bed. It's different if you win, of course, then the excitement carries you through and God only knows when the celebrations might finish. More than likely, you won't see your bed. And you can't imagine what a hangover is like after three weeks of hard racing. There's a basement club in Paris where a lot of the riders like to go, but after three weeks racing with them, they're the last people I want to see. I'm usually done with the boys at that stage. I want to see my wife.

The crits are fun because there are so many fans and it's a traditional part of cycling that I like, but it's hectic because you're driving around like crazy from race to race. Some guys do ten or eleven of them in as many days because it's such a good way to make money. Particularly if you're not one of the top riders, those couple of weeks could be the most profitable of the whole season.

The Clásica de San Sebastián in August is always good. I've already mentioned how much I like racing in the Basque Country, and after the Tour, everyone still has good legs so it's usually exciting and fast. Even for the guys who've been killing themselves at the crits. I don't think any coach could explain it, but it just seems to be that way.

The Vuelta a España can be a bit of a gamble, I think. I've had some great results there, and some terrible ones, when I was just absolutely fucked after the Tour. It's not easy to maintain your form at the top level for so long. As a race, though, I like it. The starts are later, for one thing. After the Tour, that's a welcome change. In recent years they've done more transfers, which is a pain. The first couple of times I did it, it was still very much the poor relation of the Tour and the Giro. Apart from the Spanish, the top riders mainly went as preparation for the World Championships. The only guys racing hard would be the ones without a contract for the next season. That's all changed now. You could see how much it meant to Chris Froome when he eventually won it.

THE TEAM

When you're the team leader, the pressure is intense. You don't always notice it in yourself, but you definitely change. Perhaps you have to. When I was leader I'd come to the breakfast table during a training camp or at a race, I was only worried about my food or how I felt. It didn't always occur to me to ask the other guys how they were doing or if they needed something. My whole life was blinkered like that, because everything was about the next performance and making sure I got the job done.

It's completely different now that I'm one of the older guys on the team. I'll make sure the leader has everything, maybe have a little chat about what he needs to do and how he feels, but I'm also keeping an eye on the younger guys because they need guidance. If they're eating the wrong things or if they're starting to get sick, I'll notice the signs before they do, and suggest little changes. That kind of dynamic is so important to how a team performs, but most fans never get to see it. It's part of my job now to do those things, helping the coaching staff and providing a bit of a bridge between the riders and the management.

It takes time to realise that every little detail counts. Proper training is obvious, but with experience you learn to keep a close eye on everything. To give just one example, a lot of us don't like to shake hands with strangers, especially not at the races. It sounds like hypochondria, but you don't know where they've been and something small like a fever can derail your season. In an office job, you can just stay at home for a couple of days and rest up, but if you're preparing for a big goal, it's a nightmare. Our training is so specific and planned these days that you can't just miss a few sessions without it causing a problem. And if you come down with something in the lead-up to the Tour de France and you have to pull out of the Critérium du Dauphiné, you're missing out on valuable racing time. We need that to be sharp, and that has a psychological effect on you because it's inevitable that doubts will start to creep in when you're at home sick while everyone else is out there fine-tuning themselves before the big event.

That creates a lot of stress at home. Your family definitely notice it, and that bothers me because it's not like I want to be this grumpy arsehole when I'm with them. Once my big goals are done, they see the change right away. I'll be in a better mood, more relaxed, and there's more time to play and hang out together. But coming up to a big race, there's always stress. It can feel like you're right on the edge of burning out, sometimes. Are you training enough, or too much? One can be as bad as the other. What happens when nothing seems to be working? I can remember a couple of times when I was really focused on my training and I'd lost a lot of weight, I should have been perfect, but I just felt like shit. And as you get older, you wonder: 'What's the point of this?' It's easy to think about retiring in those moments. When you're at the top of your game, the sacrifices are worth it, even when you know you're not being the best husband or father that you could be, because every minute of every day is dedicated to cycling. But you know that it's the job, it's what pays for everything, and you know that there'll be time to be a full-time family man in a few years when you're not racing any more. When nothing comes together though, you wonder what it's all for. I know a few guys think about these things a lot. You don't want your wife to be happy when you leave for a race.

Of course, every rider is different. You see some of the younger guys at the start and it looks like they haven't a care in the world. They're so cool. When I was in that position, I enjoyed it, but it weighed heavily. I also wasn't as nice as I could have been, looking back. Especially at the start. My agent was constantly telling me to stay humble and watch how I treated people, but it wasn't a natural situation for me and I struggled. That's common, though. We had one leader who would get very stressed at the big races and it would end up affecting the whole team. One year he decided he needed to lose some weight, so he went on a low-fibre diet, but out of the blue he decided that the rest of us should go low-fibre too, and he went around watching us like a policeman, shouting at soigneurs for putting the wrong kind of cereal on the breakfast table. It was weird, and potentially harmful because everyone reacts differently to diet changes like that and it could have really damaged someone's performance. One of the guys actually dared to put some Nutella on his bread one morning and he stopped him eating it and asked, 'Have you really earned that?' That's not the way to build a team when you're asking those riders to go through hell for you.

I remember getting my first iPod one year just before the Giro, and loading some films on to it to watch on that tiny little screen. I was rooming with the leader and I was afraid of upsetting him, so in the morning when I woke up I'd just watch the iPod until he got up. And at night, we'd watch the replay of the race together until 11 p.m., and then he'd have a night snack before putting on a long-sleeve top and turning off the air conditioning, no matter how hot it was. He was so regimented, and absolutely terrified of getting sick, so he'd do the same thing every evening and because I was there, I'd have to do it too. I thought that was weird at first, but then I started looking at the other guys. Some of them would eat the same dinner every night during a Grand Tour, for three weeks. And there were other riders who wouldn't eat vegetables because they'd been told that the hotel staff washed them with dirty water. The superstitions in cycling are insane. A lot of the time, alcohol only comes out when things aren't going well or when the rider doesn't really care. So towards the end of the season you'll see the big names having a beer now and then, but if they're having a shit Giro or Tour, there'll be bottles of wine at dinner. I hope I wasn't that bad.

I'm certainly different now, and when it comes to a big stage or an important time trial at a Grand Tour, I think I'm more nervous for the team leader than he is. It affects my sleep, even afterwards. It's funny, because we'll have these difficult moments at a race, perhaps mistakes are made or bad luck will hit us at the worst moment, and the rest of the day I'll be mulling it over, trying to think of what we could have done differently, how to avoid something similar next time. And the next morning, I'll see him, and he'll be as fresh as a daisy, smiling away. That's a good skill to have – a lot of races have been lost, worrying about things that couldn't be helped. He'll sit down and meticulously scrutinise what went right and wrong when the race is finished, but during it, he's focused on the coming challenge. I think that kind of concentration is a strength reserved for the lucky few guys who can afford to be confident in their talent.

There's a lot to being a road captain that doesn't always come across on TV. During a race I have to make calls when the director isn't there and I'm always feeding them back information so that they can make better decisions. I'll talk to other teams, get a feeling for the mood in the bunch, and gauge what everyone else has planned for the day. For instance, if there's a breakaway early in a stage you might want to get a rider to cover it in case it stays away, but if Marcel Kittel and

Mark Cavendish want a sprint finish, there's no need because Team Katusha–Alpecin and Team Dimension Data will do what it takes to make sure that the attack doesn't stay away. Tactically, it can be useful to spread the word around in the peloton if you're planning something. If we want to go for the win with our sprinter, I'll let the other teams know that they'll be wasting their time trying to attack early on and assuming they believe me, they could decide to try it another day instead. When it works, it's great, because you're not trying to chase down a big group of strong riders who have built up a good lead. I'm always trying to make my team's day as easy as possible.

A good captain needs some personality and it helps to have good relationships with lots of other riders. You also need a good rapport with the sports directors, because you spend more time with them than the other riders would. During a Grand Tour, one of them will come to my room every evening to discuss the next day's strategy. Not every DS will do that, but I think it's helpful for both of us. It's also crucial to be author-itative with your own teammates and to believe in the call you're making. Once I was burned for letting the leader finish having a chat before bringing him up to the front of the bunch when I was worried about crosswinds. I should have insisted and told him to phone his friend that night if it was so impor-tant to keep talking, but I let him go on and before he was done, someone had turned on the gas and the bunch was torn in two, with us in the wrong half, desperately trying to chase back on and in doing so burning through a lot of energy that we didn't need to waste. To make matters worse, when we caught up I found out that our guys hadn't realised that we weren't all together, so the ones who'd been up front had been helping to pull, trying to distance that lead group from the rest of us. It's not easy telling the star rider what to do, but that's exactly the kind of thing that could lose him a big race.

Over time, I've come to enjoy it, even though it wasn't a role that I wanted for myself originally. I like the tactical side of it now, and I love passing on some knowledge to the younger guys because no matter how talented they are, this is a different world to the one that they're used to. You have to learn how to do a Grand Tour, how to save your energy and take the best possible care of yourself. The experienced guys will always be quiet and calm, unlike most rookies, who are running around, joking with everyone. You'll see them standing around having a chat in their wet, dirty kit, thirty or forty minutes after the end of a stage, and they won't have bothered to take a recovery drink or more water. And then they'll wonder how they managed to catch a cold or why they're so exhausted by the third week. If you're a big Classics guy that might be OK, but to be a proper GC contender you always have to be thinking about the next day. The only time I've ever had a problem with the doping control people was during the Tour de France and I was called for testing right after the stage but there was no food or water there for me. I think my reaction surprised the doctor because it's not really the kind of place where you should be making a fuss, but I needed to start my recovery right away. That's what has to always come first.

Relationships between riders and staff can be very different depending on the management. Sometimes everyone's really close and sometimes they can just seem like a colleague from the other side of your office; you know them to see, but not much more than that. I like it when I can build a connection with the soigneurs and the mechanics. So much of this job is on the road, in hotels, away from family, and it's nice when you feel like you're surrounded by friendly faces. In bigger setups, that's more difficult, because there are more people and usually more protocols to follow. Riders will have a different meal time to the rest of the staff, because the directors and management will come to eat after their meetings and everyone else has a meal either after the race or getting ready for the next day. It used to be more relaxed. We were at different tables, but I always enjoyed hearing the mechanics laughing and shouting at one another over a couple of beers, because they have an incredibly hard job and it was cool to see them being positive.

Teams will also rotate through the soigneurs these days, as opposed to always having the same one like I did when I was starting out, so you don't really create the same bond there either. You might not see a soigneur for the whole Tour de France, for instance. If you're not on his table, you won't see him at breakfast or dinner, so with the possible exception of a team meeting, you never cross paths.

Some teams struggle, particularly at the beginning of the season, with new mechanics. And the main reason is just that they don't want to spend money on experienced guys. There are always a few riders in the bunch who will be a little grumpy during the early races like the Dubai Tour, because gears will be mis-shifting and tyres will be rubbing. The poor junior mechanic more than likely gets the blame for that, but they're doing their best and it wouldn't happen if the management spent more money trying to keep the experienced ones. You need experience to train up the newbies, instead of leaving them with this crazy steep learning curve, trying to take care of a team full of extremely fussy riders. Most of the time, the good ones only hang on for a few years, and then they go off to do something else. They want to try something more fun and be closer to home. I can't blame them, either, because their wages are shit and they're expected to work crazy hours and spend most of the year away from home.

That penny-pinching is felt by everyone. When it comes to expenses, cycling teams can be almost comically cheap. We could win a huge stage at a Grand Tour, but at the dinner that night, wine might be too expensive. Or a rider could be going from one race to another, and when he gets his itinerary from the team, it will involve two or three slow trains and a load of waiting, when there's a high-speed train or a direct flight available. I know most guys will end up just paying for the quicker option out of their own pocket, because no one wants to be sitting around a train station all day, or making a journey that takes six hours when it could only take two.

My current team has some amazing equipment, and I can say this honestly because you don't know who I am and I'm not promoting anything. I love the frame and I think the wheels and groupsets are awesome, I've never had a problem. But that's not worth much if the mechanic looking after it doesn't know how to maintain things properly. Particularly when it comes to the time-trial bikes, they have to be perfect, and there's no room for error. Every cyclist knows how annoying it is to be out on a ride, only to find that his bike is not shifting gear quickly or he can hear the squeal of brake pads. That's a pain if you're out training or on a weekend spin with your club, but in a racing situation it's a serious problem. If your chain is skipping when you try to shift on a relaxed ride, you might adjust the cable tension while rolling along, or just live with it. Once you're not pushing really hard, the skipping isn't going to be such a big issue. In a time trial, however, it has to be *perfect*. You can't ease off the gas, and the last thing you want to hear is the screech of brake pads because you need to be 100 per cent confident in the stopping distance.

In the early part of the season, the big Grand Tour riders won't do a lot of races, they'll have a few key events that they want to perform well at before concentrating on their main target of that year, either the Giro d'Italia in May or the Tour de France in July. Racing in the spring helps with fitness later in the year, but there is also a lot of work that goes into being ready for those specific races and if you fly out to Dubai or Abu Dhabi only to find that the new mechanic can't get your equipment right and your TT bike has rubbing tyres and doesn't shift properly, it's demoralising because all of that work before and after Christmas will have been for nothing.

It's hard because we can't come out complaining about the team in that situation. We can blame it on a mechanical, but that makes it sound like a freak occurrence rather than something that could, and should, have been prevented. It's not the mechanics' fault anyway. They're underpaid and they're asked to do too much. All of the staff are. Unless you're one of the WorldTour teams with a huge budget – Team Sky, Katusha–Alpecin, BMC Racing – you'll see a lot of them doing two completely different jobs, or at least bogged down with a heavy workload. It's worse as you go down the rankings, on a Pro Continental team the bus driver might also be a soigneur, or the doctor could moonlight as a chiropractor. But cutbacks are happening everywhere. I know that some teams are cutting down on massage times, for example, so fewer staff can look after more riders. It's smart to watch the finances like that, but only up to a point. The soigneurs have a demanding job, and a proper massage is physically draining. You see them sometimes, rubbing their hands, or if you're the last guy on the schedule, maybe your masseuse won't have the strength to work the really deep muscles the way he'd like to.

It used to feel like we knew one another, and I've actually invited some of the staff from old teams to family functions because they had become friends. I don't think that would happen on a lot of the big teams today, apart from maybe Quick-Step because those guys are old school and all seem very close, but I make an effort to connect when I can. I think little gestures are important, so I'll drop a six-pack of beers down with the service course every so often to say thanks and show them that I'm grateful for what they do. A few beers go a long way. It's the right thing to do, because those mechanics work their arses off for me and the other riders. A six-pack and a little chat shows that I'm not totally ignorant of all their efforts. And if you take the time, as a happy coincidence, you'll always be the first guy to get fresh bar tape. I don't want to sound like an old grump, whingeing on, but I worry that the younger generation of riders don't appreciate how important the overall team is to their success. I was brought up to think of the team, the soigneurs and the mechanics, as almost a family, so it was always a big thing for me to make some time to hang out with them or to at least pop by with a few beers and say thanks for all the hard work.

That kind of thing is less common than it was ten years ago, but probably just because there was less to do back then. You were in some soulless hotel in the middle of nowhere in a foreign country, so unless you wanted to watch TV in a language you didn't understand, you'd hang around after dinner to have a coffee or a beer with everyone else and talk. Nowadays you can just go to your room and video call your girlfriend or watch a movie. It's easier to create your own little bubble. On my first team one of the riders used to bring headphones to listen to his own music and we all thought he was super rude because we listened to whatever someone put on the bus's stereo. It would be weird if someone came without headphones now.

We used to hang out more, play cards. And it's embarrassing to say it now, but porn was a really big thing too. Everyone would bring magazines and they'd share them around. Looking back on it, the guys who were most into that were probably really into using testosterone too, so it makes sense that they'd be horny all the time.

We had the team presentation downtown a few seasons ago, it was a nice hotel, in the middle of the city. It was the day before our first training camp of the year, but everyone was in their rooms by ten o'clock, no one went out for a drink. I thought it was a bit pathetic. I was the same, of course, but I have an excuse, I'm one of the old riders, I've reached that age when going to bed early actually sounds appealing. But back when I was in my early twenties, I'd have been excited to explore a bit and have some fun with my teammates. I'm not talking about a ten-hour drinking binge, just an hour or two shooting the shit and having a laugh together. It feels a bit like cycling has been neutered these days. I love that everyone trains so hard and wants to compete, but I don't think a few beers in January is going to hurt you at the Giro or the Tour. In fact, I've always thought that things like that can help a team, because you're more likely to go to hell and back for a leader that you like than for some guy you hardly know. I don't mean to say that we're not always trying, but you'll work harder when there's a bond, that's just human nature. If you're at an early season race, you might still catch a guy like Pippo Pozzato in a bar somewhere. He knows when to do it, of course, and you shouldn't let his image as a party boy fool you because he's a real pro, but I like seeing a guy who can balance normal life with cycling. It's not normal to live like a monk 365 days a year. And if I was a director, I'd be happy with a rider like that, because he's got personality, he's popular, and I'm sure he sells more stuff for the sponsors than the rest of the team combined.

I've been on teams that had the joy sucked out of them by stress. It's awful. One of the guys could go win a stage at a Grand Tour and it would barely register with the staff because they're so over-worked and tense. One of the best things about my current team is that they try to enjoy the ride. If you've ever been around a WorldTour team, you'll know how difficult that can be because of the pressure, the travel, and the long hours, but it's important to try. Something as simple as a group dinner or a barbecue on the rest day at a big race can make all the difference. The Basque team, Euskaltel–Euskadi, was famous for that. You can mingle, out of the context of the team, and get to know people. If you're only focused on the race and your results, you'd never know that the doctor really loves to cook or that the soigneur is a major craft-beer buff. A team shouldn't feel like a group of strangers.

In general, the old familial feeling is gone. All that matters now are results and executing the plan set out by the management. They're not paying you to be pals or to be happy. That's not to say that they want us to be miserable, not at all, it's just that favours and personalities don't really matter any more. Once upon a time, even if you were being a bit of a pain in the arse, if something was important to you, you could ask, and the manager would try to accommodate you. Now, if it's not on the spreadsheet, it's not happening. I was asked to ride at a local time-trial event near my home a while ago, and I was delighted to go, but when I asked the team for my proper TT bike, I was dismissed right away. I couldn't even borrow a pair of aero wheels. They're right, obviously, it's a business and everything has to be accounted for, and I'm only one of many riders, but they shouldn't want one of their WorldTour stars showing up to an amateur time trial without the proper kit, either. At that TT, I think I was the only one there without a disc wheel, because it's not like I could use any old thing I had in my shed. I had to think of the sponsors, even if they weren't thinking of me.

EQUIPMENT

If you want to know the truth about the latest equipment, don't ask a pro. At least not one that's speaking on the record. We're told what to use and we have to be positive about it, even when it sucks. It's been that way since the beginning of the sport. And while I've been in the game for a long time now, it is still surprising to see how bad some gear can be. I don't know how the manufacturers stay in business. Around a decade ago, Vittoria tyres should have come with a health warning for wet conditions, and I've seen plenty of companies pushing 'aero' products that should have seen them sued for false advertising.

One year at the Tour de France, our tyres were incredibly shit in the rain. I definitely envied the teams riding Continental, because they just looked so much more comfortable in the wet. I can remember it raining on a couple of the big descents and being left for dead by Mark Cavendish and Bernhard Eisel – both of whom were using Contis. On at least one of those occasions I had a good lead on them going over the top – the sprinters take it easy in the mountains and just focus on getting to the end of the stage – but after ten kilometres they were able to fly by me. I'm not a bad descender but I just couldn't keep up.

I think they told us that it was a bad batch, something wrong with the rubber, but that doesn't change much. Whatever the cause, they still sucked and they still cost the team dearly. Our GC hopes were dashed by a couple of crashes that I'd blame squarely on the tyres, and when you have no confidence in the rubber beneath you, in the grip that's holding you to the road, you're never going to be able to push yourself to the limit on the downhill. With good tyres that I trust, I never even think about it, but when you know something isn't right, it feels suicidal.

I've said before that pro riders have short memories. It's a blessing and a curse. It makes it easier to get over crashes and to put up with the gruelling hours spent out training, but it also means that we're liable to repeat silly mistakes. Everyone on the team cursed those tyres at the time, but a year or two later, an old teammate told me a funny story. He was packing all his stuff into the car for a busy crit season, when he came across a pair of that season's aero wheels, which he really liked. Most equipment suppliers won't let you take things like that home for your own events, so this was a result. And better yet, they had a brand-new set of tubulars on them. He thought it was a stroke of good luck, until midway through one crit when it started pouring down with rain. He'd had a good season, so as one of the big attractions, the organiser was expecting him to win, or at least place highly.

As I'm sure everybody knows, the summertime criteriums after the Tour de France aren't exactly Corinthian in spirit. The most charitable way of putting it is that the organisers give the crowds what they want. My buddy had a good season, which meant he was getting good appearance fees, but it also meant that everyone was expecting him to be at the front. As soon as the road got a bit damp, however, he was filled with dread because all the old memories came flooding back and he spent the next few laps cursing either himself or the tyre manufacturer in the few moments when he wasn't skidding around the place.

I was laughing while he told me this because I could picture it perfectly, you could hardly go around a corner on those things in the wet, let alone keep up with the rest of the bunch on a tight criterium course. On a quiet part of the course, he stopped to let some air out to see if that would improve things, but it didn't work so when he re-joined the front group when they came around again, he had to come clean to the other riders. He apologised, explained that the organiser was expecting to see him on the podium, and then told them that he could barely get his bike around the bends. Luckily, the other guys all knew the drill, so they all came up with a way to make it look believable that he could stay in the bunch in spite of the handicap, and at the finish, they let him come third. Only in professional cycling.

More recently, my team showed up to training camp with a fresh batch of some new prototype tyres for us to test. I was so pissed off. They spent all this money on putting together a team of expensive, and fragile, professional athletes and then they ask us to act like crash test dummies. I don't know why the manufacturers don't do the testing themselves – see how they like it when they keep falling on their arses. I'd love for them to explain the thinking behind that to me. It's good for marketing to say that this or that has been rigorously tested by the pros, but the reality is that a machine in a laboratory could give you a more accurate appraisal at a fraction of the cost and hassle. And what happens if something shitty causes all of our riders to crash? One of our main guys came off at a training camp earlier in the year because of some new tyres, and it left him with some niggling injuries. As a result, he couldn't ride his bike for a few weeks. Aside from the fact that I think asking anyone to push an untried product to its limits is a dickhead move, even looked at dispassionately, we're simply too expensive to risk like that. What genius thought it would be a good idea to risk an injury to an employee who they pay millions of euros to ride his bike? That salary is a total waste if he's sitting in a hospital bed, or back on his couch at home, watching TV instead of training.

I'd love to talk to one of the riders from the Aqua Blue Sport team about a lot of things – the way that team ended was a sad indictment of our sport – but even before they went bust, their equipment setup in 2018 shocked me, because they were riding a bike from 3T that was designed to work with SRAM's 1x groupset. We've all grown up riding two chainrings up front and I'd hate to have a change like that forced upon me by sponsors. I can imagine some very strong language coming from my teammates when the news broke. I'd probably start making jokes about retirement.

Unusually, there were complaints creeping out of the Aqua Blue camp even *before* the team collapsed, so things must have really been bad. Public criticism of the sponsors or any deviation from the official line is typically met with the kind of response that would make a Soviet-era secret policeman proud, but I remember Adam Blythe, one of the more experienced riders on the ream, openly joking about it being a track bike with gears stuck onto it, because it was so poorly suited to road racing. And they had so many mechanical problems that even the team boss, Rick Delaney, seemed to regret his decision. I saved one tweet from him at the Tour de Suisse:

'Just want to say what a privilege it was to be behind @ MarkChristian8 today @tds so so strong, only to be dropped by mechanical no 4698 this season ... This lab rat thing is now costing results. sorry again Mark!'

Lab rats is exactly what they were, and my teammates and I would not have been amused, to put it mildly. I don't think the decision was made with any racing justification, it was purely motivated by money, to grab headlines for a sponsor with cash to spend. Which is not to say I dislike the idea of having a single chainring. It's lighter, you'll never drop a chain again, and it's easier to maintain. For a cyclocross, mountain bike and gravel, that's great. It's so much easier to keep it all clean. But for us, riding up and down mountains, I don't see how it can be as good as a traditional crankset. I have 53-tooth and 39-tooth chainrings to match up with an 11-speed cassette, which these days might go as high as 28-, 30-, or even 32-tooth. I know a couple of guys who like using a semi-compact crank up front, which has a smaller 36-tooth chainring for some really easy climbing gears. That's a lot of variation, and I don't see how one chainring can provide that same experience. For one thing, there'll be bigger jumps between the gears and that has to mess with your cadence. I like having a close range so that I can always find the perfect gear for my rhythm. The Aqua Blue riders must have been shifting like crazy trying to find the sweet spot, and considering how modern racing is so closely linked to specific power outputs, I don't see how eleven sprockets on the back can compare to the range we have with traditional double chainrings. Sprinters like Larry Warbasse were riding 9- to 32-tooth cassettes, which might be OK, aside from the fact that I think there must be a good reason why other manufacturers only go as low as 11 teeth, but the climbers were on 9 to 52 and that seems crazy. The low and high ends might be the same as a traditional groupset, but in between you're making huge sacrifices. Most people who've been riding for a long time started out on straight blocks – each gear increases by one – and in a racing context I can't imagine being able to compensate for that change.

When I'm no longer racing, it will be a different story – I can definitely see myself having one. And for my wife, it's great, because she doesn't ride all that much and it's simpler to just have one shifter to think about. She doesn't want the extra hassle of thinking about ratios and cadence, but she's not racing a Grand Tour. Purely in the context of professional racing, the only reason I can see for using the 1x system is because SRAM want to sell product. I don't mean that in a cynical way, either. That's their business, and it makes sense to show the public the kind of equipment that might actually improve their cycling experience. I've thought that for years, I don't understand why some companies still want to sell race bikes to a casual rider. It makes no sense, because the bikes we ride in the bunch have changed a lot in recent years, getting more and more specialised. Back in the day, one frame could do it all – you just changed the wheels or tyres to suit your riding style. There was space for mudguards to keep the spray out of the faces of your friends on wet rides, and usually you'd find some way to attach racks and pannier bags the odd time you fancied going bike-packing. You might have another bike for cyclocross and a mountain bike, but the average cyclist didn't have a fleet of bikes like so many do today. And if they did, it was because they liked collecting them, rather than any particular need.

These days it's not unusual to have four or five bikes for different disciplines, such as gravel riding, racing, or touring. But I think it's stupid to have to chop and change between different bikes if you don't want to, so I love to see anything like the 3T frames or the 1x groupsets that could create a more versatile, fun machine. In the case of the single chainrings, there's an aerodynamic improvement as well, but that area of the bike is so busy with bottle cages, cranks, pedals, and legs, that I'm not convinced the lack of a front derailleur is going to make a massive difference outside of a wind tunnel. Anyway, I like that it's different and that they're trying to introduce new ways of thinking into the peloton – I'm just glad they called someone else's team to do it.

The most annoying things can actually be the little details, like the bike computer. You could be with Garmin one year, and then Wahoo or Sigma the next. It seems petty to complain about it, but I hate settings those things up, trying to figure out the maps, connecting it properly to the power meter, stuff like that. I just want to ride my bike.

It's one of the things I'll look forward to most about retirement: being able to use whatever the hell I want. Not getting phone calls from someone who's upset with me because I wasn't sponsor-correct on social media, and being able to use one brand for on the road and another brand for mountain biking or gravel rides. The 2018 Strade Bianche was a great example – a lot of riders were just sent out with whatever their teams conceived to be the best option. There was no discussion, even though they were asking us to ride ourselves ragged in rotten conditions on some really technical terrain. The white gravel roads that make that part of Tuscany famous are testing at the best of times, but after hard rain like we had in 2018, they're genuinely treacherous. Which is what we all love about it – it makes for exciting, unpredictable, difficult racing. No one is ever going to fluke their way to a victory in a race like that. But it's crazy how little consultation some teams give their riders.

For some context, the organisers run a granfondo for the amateurs on the same weekend and almost everyone who was serious about the event was on big tyres. I'm not even talking about proper gravel bikes – a small change from 25 to 27 or 28 millimetres still makes an enormous difference. These days the majority of the peloton is on 25mm for much of the year, but at the start line in Siena, you could see that while most of the teams had wisely elected for bigger rubber, not everyone was willing to make the effort. More than likely, that's a know-it-all manager sitting behind a desk somewhere, refusing to change his plan despite the changing conditions and, I'd imagine, some vociferous rider protest. It's certainly not the sponsor's call because the last thing they want to see is one of their teams struggling for grip. That would make them look bad, and stupid, too, because all of the tyre manufacturers have a wide range of tyre sizes. It's not like Vittoria or Continental didn't think to make a 28mm model. The previous years had been dry and 25mm was OK for that, so they just stuck to what they knew. It's a typical attitude for cycling – we've always done it like this, so we'll keep doing it like this. For us riders, when something like that happens, it can feel like you've lost before you've even begun. The psychological blow is probably bigger than the actual performance deficit, but there is a definite drop-off in terms of performance. Riding in the dirt or in sand, it's all about the tyre pressure and the width. You can be the best bike handler in the world and it won't matter if you're on the wrong tyres because you won't have any grip. Those poor guys on the 25mm tyres were sinking into sections of mud that the rest of us were just riding over. They had no chance.

I've been lucky with most of the frames I've ridden, but at almost every race I'll see someone who I feel genuinely sorry for because I know what it's like to be stuck on a terrible bike. During my best years, I think my time-trial bike cost me at least a place or two in every stage race, every time. It was a real piece of shit. The first time I got into the top ten in a Grand Tour, I did the most important TT of my life on a frame that had just arrived from the factory. I'd never seen it before, but they'd delivered it specially because even they knew that the previous one they'd given me was terrible. I had my local bike fitter flown in to get me as comfortable as possible, and he made the best of a bad situation, but it was a joke. Look at how long we spend in wind tunnels nowadays, perfecting our position and overall aerodynamics. And it changes based on little things like helmets and clothing. Now imagine what kind of effect sticking a rider on a brand-new frame is going to have. I was woeful in that TT, and it wasn't because of form because the days leading up to it, I was flying in the mountains, no one was able to drop me. When we did more testing on that model, you could see how soft it was in the back because the tyres were rubbing against the stays.

That was kept quiet, of course. It wouldn't do for any of us to ever speak openly or honestly about the equipment we're riding every day. If you ask Michał Kwiatkowski or Geraint Thomas, they'll tell you that Pinarello make the best bikes. Taylor Phinney will swear by Cannondale. Marcel Kittel would have insisted it was Specialized, until he moved to Team Katusha–Alpecin for the 2018 season and started riding Canyon. I'm the same. The whole peloton is. We ride whatever we're paid to, and part of the gig is singing praises whenever we're asked about a product. It's a part of cycling, but it's very rarely honest. I'm constantly surprised by the fact that some companies stay in business, because the gulf between them and their competition is enormous. Some 'aero' wheels are so slow you don't need a wind tunnel to test them, you can feel the difference just by freewheeling. I've worn glasses that were more of a hinderance than a help, either fogging up entirely as soon as you put them on, or almost blinding you, thanks to ventilation holes that seemed like they were designed for the sole purpose of channelling high-pressure jets of air right onto your pupils. A lot of the processed energy products like bars and gels are inedible in all but the most desperate of situations, which is why riders get genuinely excited by the prospect of a good team chef or a nutritionist. So whenever you see or hear a glowing review of a product from a pro, take it with a pinch of salt, and the next time you're wondering how a certain rider suddenly got so good – or bad – at time trialling or descending, take a minute to check that his team hasn't just changed sponsor.

CONTRACTS AND AGENTS

It takes a special kind of person to want to be a professional cyclist. If you have another opportunity, such as university, you really have to think long and hard about it, because unless you're very talented, you're not going to make a fortune racing bikes.

Back when I was getting into it, anyone who didn't have that alternative was in a vulnerable place; if all they had was cycling, then I think the pressure of that unfortunately led to a lot of people making bad decisions and doing things like doping that they didn't really want to do. Guys like Lance Armstrong got the headlines, but there were people using performance-enhancing drugs just to hang on to contracts that were worth what people working in business somewhere would think of as a very average salary. But without an education to fall back on, keeping a spot on a team as a domestique and earning €60,000 a year was a lot more than they could make anywhere else. I raced with people in the amateur ranks who could have turned professional quite easily, some of them might even have become quite famous, but they weighed up their options and chose to study instead because ultimately it's a more secure future.

This life is a gamble. These days it's easier to get identified as a talent early on, the sport is becoming more international and better organised – that wouldn't be hard, because it was a circus – than it was twenty years ago. News travels faster, travel is easier, and the racing scene isn't as regional as it was when I was young. If you're good, your national team should get you to bigger races and there are more, and better, development teams, so you can compete against the best in your age group. The culture has changed in the big teams, too, and now they want to invest in young talent. That's not always for altruistic reasons – it's just a lot cheaper to sign a guy young and hope he makes it big before you have to give him a huge contract. A lot of young riders get snapped up now after a year or two in the Under-23 category because there's a market for them among the bigger teams. Teams these days are trying to buy a future. It's probably a question of budgets, the sport is getting more expensive to operate within, but there's still a fairly limited pool of potential investment, and it makes sense for a team to hire a couple of promising neo-pros for the minimum wage rather than having two older guys on the books who expect more money because they need to cover their bottom lines. As of 2018 there was an increase in that minimum: from January 2018, neo-pros get at least €25,806 at Pro Continental level and €30,839 on a WorldTour team. Salaries for older riders begin at €30,855 at Pro Continental and €38,115 on the WorldTour. That's not bad for a kid who still lives at home and who's dreaming of making it big doing something he loves, especially if you're from somewhere like Italy or Spain where the cost of living isn't that high. Also, the youth unemployment rates in those countries is above 30 per cent, so getting the chance to be a pro cyclist must seem like winning the lottery to some of them. And you're with the team most of the time, they cover your expenses, you're not buying kit or anything like that, so if you live for cycling and you can make even that minimum wage as a twenty-one-year-old, it's not a bad life.

Obviously, it goes without saying that it is not a lot of cash for a guy with a family to support, especially not when he's trying to plan for the rest of his life after retirement. I don't think anyone at this level should be making less than €60,000 a year. Eighty is comfortable enough to make it worthwhile. When you're young, the money shouldn't really come into it. If you're talented, you'll get your fair share. I've been around long enough to say that the rumours you hear about guys getting ripped off, or being manipulated by teams, are for the most part untrue. There's a lot of bitter ex-riders out there who feel hard done by, but ultimately it's market driven.

The caveat to that is that you need a good agent. And by good, I mean someone who is qualified and professional, who has your best interests at heart. A lot of agents will just work within their own little networks, and no matter who the rider is, they'll only do business with maybe three or four teams, because that's where the agent has relationships. But if those relationships are too concentrated, it's going to limit the athlete's opportunities. At the same time, it's not like every athlete is going to be good on every team. There are teams that do a great job developing young talent, and there are teams that do a horrible job. There are also riders who will prosper regardless, and really talented kids who need the right environment. If I was an agent, I'd be most concerned about finding the right place to nurture the rider's potential. If that's done correctly, you'll make the big money a couple of years down the road when he's the finished product and can actually demand a big contract.

You might look at a massive outfit like Team Sky and think that they'd be a bad fit for a young rider, but it really depends on the kid. It's true that they hire big talents and end up turning them into domestiques or peripheral characters. They've done that with everyone from Mark Cavendish, who had to play second fiddle at the Tour de France to Brad Wiggins' ambitions, to Mikel Landa, who made a big splash at the 2015 Giro d'Italia with Astana and then ended up spending two frustrating years someway down the Sky pecking order before moving to Movistar. But those guys were on big contracts and they went there with the belief that they were good enough to become the star. Having a lot of talent on the roster and sticking with a proven winner is not the same thing as being bad at developing potential. If I was a young British rider with a lot of promise and enough self-confidence to stand on my own two feet in that kind of illustrious company, I would definitely want to go there (current doping accusations notwithstanding). Guys like Geraint Thomas and Ian Stannard have been there since they were young and have done really well, Luke Rowe has developed well, and though he's only twenty-two, Tao Geoghegan Hart looks like he has a bright future. And all have certainly progressed without a hint of suspicion. On the other hand, if you don't speak English well and you're not ready to live up to that team's super-planned, pedantic approach to everything, it's going to be a bad fit for you. Quick-Step do a good job too, and Team Sunweb. At those top teams, the pressure will be high, but they're great schools, you're going to get a brilliant education in how to become a top professional rider.

There are a lot of things that other teams do wrong. Sometimes it can feel a bit like the Wild West rather than a modern professional sport. Everyone's looking after number one, which usually means that someone else is getting fucked over. Look again at what happened to Aqua Blue Sport. They set out to be this self-sustaining team, with revenue coming from an online cycling shop. It was a really nice idea and it sounded like someone was actually trying to be innovative and thoughtful for once. But after only two years, they folded. There were rumours that they'd merge with another Pro Continental team but that didn't work out, and if you believe what you read online, some of the riders only found out about their demise on Twitter, because I saw Andrew Fenn's partner talking about it on social media.

It's not always as dramatic as that, but even the top teams regularly do things that I don't think they should be doing. For instance, most teams right now just don't have enough riders to cover the whole calendar, so they'll send a guy to a race last minute, even if they're a bit sick or injured, knowing that they're going to drop out immediately. They'll be fined if they can't produce a full squad at the start, so the solution is to fly someone over and let them drop out after a few kilometres just to avoid a fine of six or seven thousand euros. The call could come two days before the race. If you're smart, you could pretend to be sick, but that's not very professional and it's not something I'd do. If they need me, I'll always go, but I don't think they should be asking.

The last time they made me drop everything a few days before the start of a big race, when they were booking my flight they bought a return ticket, knowing I'd be back home at the end of the first day. That sucks for the rider, who should be given enough respect to enjoy his scheduled time off, or be allowed to recuperate in comfort at home, but it's also totally unfair on the race organisers because they're paying the teams to show up. They just want to collect that start money and then think of some excuse, even though they had already booked return flights before the race even began. It's probably not the worst thing that goes on in the grand scheme of things, but it gives you a good idea about the general attitude. It's dog eat dog, and to hell with the other guys.

It's the same with the transfer market. Unless you're a big name, everyone is waiting for the fire sale so they can get everyone cheap. In the summer of 2018, you saw that with BMC. There were no big moves, because all of the teams were waiting for BMC to fall apart so they could get one or two of their guys on the cheap. Looked at coldly, that's good business for the teams, but it's terrible on the riders because their futures were hanging in the balance. The Polish team CCC–Sprandi–Polkowice ended up coming in to save the day, but it could easily have gone the other way. Maybe that's not such a big problem if you're Richie Porte, Rohan Dennis, or Greg Van Avermaet, because they're good enough to get a job anywhere, but it's not so easy for the domestiques – not to mention all of the mechanics and soigneurs.

The biggest challenge for a rider is at the beginning. For the first few years, all you want is to absorb as much as you can and adapt to the WorldTour level because no matter how good you are as an amateur, nothing prepares you for that step up. Talent at that age earns you the right to a shot: it's an opportunity, not an entitlement. You might make it, you might be washed out in two years. If you can make that adaptation and prove your worth to a team, there'll be a big jump in your next contract. You could go from €50,000 to €200,000 in the space of two years if you show promise. You need to prove that you have the potential to earn a bump like that, but you don't need to go out and win big your first year. A good team will be planning for you to come good at twenty-five or twenty-six, but with the money, there will also be bigger expectations. Some guys don't understand that and they'll take a lucrative deal from a team because it looks attractive, when actually it would have been better for them to stay settled, earn a little less, and work hard on improving. Managers are willing to pay when they see talent, but the rider needs to understand that they will expect a return on that investment. No one is paying high six-figure salaries for water carriers that get dropped the second the race gets going. I don't want to imply that Taylor Phinney is like that because he's hugely talented and he's had some serious injuries to contend with, but it was rumoured that he was on six figures while still technically an amateur, and when he signed for BMC, his neo-pro contract was around $500,000. That's an insane amount of money for a rider who hadn't even turned twenty-one, and I can't help but wonder if that pressure ended up stunting his development long-term.

When that goes wrong, you'll see guys retire and then spend their time on social media talking about how they got fucked by the system or cheated by their team managers. They have my sympathies, but that's not the system's fault. If you couldn't keep your spot, you weren't up to the challenge. It bears repeating that this is an opportunity, nothing more. If a team sees something in a rider who's riding domestically in the US for a Continental team, that's an amazing opening for him, but it's also a very steep learning curve because compared to the kind of races he's used to, racing with Professional Continental and WorldTour teams is almost a different sport. The difference between someone who races at that level and a European pro is night and day. There's a job for a rider like that on every team, but there are also 100 or 200 guys who could do it just as well. Getting that shot ahead of all the others might mean that you've got some unrealised potential that the team has seen, or it might just mean that you got lucky. So if he can't ride that luck, it's not the system's fault, that's just the nature of elite-level sport. If you talk about Alberto Contador, Peter Sagan, Alejandro Valverde – they are one of a kind. That's it, it's that guy, and he'll make millions because of it. As you go down the pyramid though, the dynamics change. Perhaps there are twenty top-level riders who, on their day, can challenge for a stage win for the mountains or the Classics, and all the big teams will want a couple of those. For the reliable domestiques who can work hard every day at a Grand Tour, there might be fifty or sixty, and so on. By the time you get to the lowest ranked support rider, there are hundreds. And I'm not saying that disrespectfully, because at different times in my career I've been almost all of these guys. But there are riders who are working at the beginning, getting bottles and food, going back and forth to the cars, and by the time the race really starts, when the pace increases and the helicopters start hovering above to let you know that everyone at home is watching, he's shot out the back of the bunch. On a big mountain pass, he'll come over the line half an hour behind, because he's been working at the start, doing the kind of things that the public doesn't usually see. It's an important job, but you don't need a very specialist skillset to do it. That's why I'm never sure if I think it's funny or annoying when people quit and talk about how unfairly they were treated. Those guys are bitter, when they should be grateful. I know that for every moaning retiree out there, there are hundreds of good bike riders who would have done anything to just get the opportunity to ride a big race once in their lives.

I love seeing riders go the opposite way. Someone like Ted King, who retired in 2015, had a good career and I don't know anyone who didn't like him. That kind of rider is primarily a bricklayer for the team, but Ted went out and laid the bricks straight so that his teammates could come along after and build on his foundation. He never complained, even when he got disqualified because of a bullshit rule in his debut Tour de France – he crashed and finished the first stage time trial with a separated shoulder but seven seconds outside of the cut-off time. He told his story honestly and he built up a sizeable following of loyal fans on social media that I'd imagine did him no harm when he was negotiating contracts. It's cool when you see riders embrace what they've been given and build on that, and these days you can use platforms like Twitter, Strava, or Zwift to create your own brand directly with the fans – do it well and that's going to make a difference to your paycheque.

It's hard to know what other riders like me are on, but when you see half a team living in Monaco, you get a good enough idea about the kind of salaries they're paying. And when you're riding along, you'll overhear some of them chatting about getting a helicopter to Nice airport because it's quicker than a cab and it only costs a couple of hundred euros, while the guy beside them might have to save a receipt and wait a month to be reimbursed for a €10 train ticket. For that reason, I think that's why some managers prefer to build a team with up-and-coming talents, where the unit is always more important than the individual. It prevents any of the precious carry-on because there's not one big star. Everyone just does as they're told.

I've also known guys who were legally declaring themselves as resident in Monaco, when they were in fact living elsewhere. Every few weeks, they'd drive to Monte Carlo and take out crazy amounts of cash so that they didn't have to use their cards anywhere else to pay for things. You'd go into a guy's apartment and there'd be a couple of grand in €50 notes sitting in the fruit bowl.

I doubt most fans appreciate the reality of cycling's pay structure. It's not just about your past results or your name, there are so many factors. Some riders will earn less than they could because they want more control over their schedules, for example. If you don't want to be away all year, you need to find the team that will work with you on that, which is going to limit your options on the market.

I've always tried to strike the balance because I knew it would lengthen my career, so I probably haven't earned as much as I could have, because I never wanted to say yes to everything just for a cheque. It's funny to think now how easy it was to spend the money when I had my biggest contract, and I don't think I was ever flash, but if you're making €20,000 or €30,000 net a month, you don't really think twice about things like first-class plane tickets. Now I have to, because a round trip might cost my whole paycheque. But even if I used to make fifteen or twenty times what I make now, this last year has been the happiest of my career, and that's not something you can easily put a figure on. Outside of the context of professional sports, I'm still a young guy, I have savings, I've invested in property that I was able to pay for upfront. There's not a lot to complain about.

If I lived in Monaco, I'd want to shoot myself. I'm not into that kind of life, and it would bug the hell out of me to pay five or six euros for an espresso every time I went to a bar. Even the fancy people would be hard for me to endure, I like going out in my jeans and a T-shirt and not caring too much. Maybe they wear casual stuff too, but their trainers cost ten times what mine do. And the thought of paying €15,000 a month in rent ... I know some guys do and with the money they're saving in tax, maybe it's worth it, but the simple life, close to home, suits me more. There are a few small cities in Spain and Italy that might have worked for me, but my wife never wanted to live there and I never wanted to get divorced, so it was an easy decision to make.

When I decided to bin the idea of moving somewhere for tax reasons, a friend of mine told me that it was the best financial decision I'd ever made, because a happy home life would extend my career and I'd end up making more money anyway. The tax thing is a big issue and I'm sure some guys will read this and think I'm an idiot, but I never made my decisions based on that. If you like living in Andorra or Monaco, good for you, but I like seeing my family and friends. Any couple that has a professional athlete in it is going to have to work together to limit the stresses because it's such a crazy and demanding lifestyle. So having your husband or wife unhappy at home isn't going to work, because they'll keep complaining about the situation and asking you about retirement, or giving you grief about your training schedule. I can ride my bike anywhere, and I travel so much anyway that my wife's happiness was the main factor in us choosing a place to buy a home.

More than likely, it's the same with a lot of professional athletes, but certainly in cycling you get two different types of people: those who like to live fast and burn through money, and those who are totally focused on coming out the other end of their careers with something in the bank to show for it. It's strange, but both character traits are typical of someone who gets to this level. There's not usually much middle ground in anything you do: either you love something and you go 100 per cent at it, or you invest your energies elsewhere. My goal was always to build a life for myself while the good times lasted, so I bought a house, invested a little. I was like that as a kid, too. Other guys would get a little prize money from a criterium or something and they'd be in town the next day, buying designer clothes. With me, I might not bother to buy a pair of jeans for two or three years, but if I got money, I'd save for something special, I was always setting long-term goals.

A good agent can help a rider with that stuff. Fundamentally, they need to do three things. First, they need to get the rider an opportunity to turn professional. If you're good enough, you've won a stage at the Tour de l'Avenir or you're a junior or U-23 world champion, you don't need an agent for that, you'll get picked up, but for most of us, that's not the starting point and a good agent needs to make a convincing case for you being good enough to warrant a spot on a team. And regardless of how good you are, the agent will help you choose the right contract. Most of the time it's fairly standard, but there's always things in there that can get tricky, whether it's side deals with other sponsors or deciding what kind of things the team can use you for away from racing, like sponsor events.

Secondly, a good agent needs to be constantly making sure that the athlete is maximising his or her earning potential. If I'm trying to concentrate on training, racing, family, I don't have time to worry about doing some deal with a shoe company in Germany or a cereal brand in France. The agent should have a plan for the athlete to make sure they're at the top of their game by twenty-five or twenty-six in terms of sporting and financial performance, while also guiding you around the usual mistakes young people make when they earn a lot of money. A career might be seven years, or it could be fifteen, the goal is making sure that you make every cent you can from it because you'll be coming out the other end in your thirties with a life ahead of you and having to start all over. My agent has always made sure that I'm careful with money, that I'm not wasting it on frivolous things and that I'm saving enough, that I've made good investments. If I buy a car, I'll talk to him about it. If I really want it, I'll buy it, but he's a smart guy and I trust him, so if he thinks it's a bad call it will give me pause for thought. Younger riders might still live at home and they might not have any real expenses, so on paper it looks OK to them to walk into a dealership and buy a €60,000 car, but they should have someone watching out for that kind of spending. The money we're making can look impressive when you're in your early twenties, but we're not earning like that for forty or fifty years like a normal person.

And lastly, a good agent should be able to help with the transition from pro athlete to normal citizen. That reintegration to society can be really hard, because nothing about being a pro athlete teaches you how to behave in the normal world, how to be a decent person, someone who contributes to their community, and who thinks about other people. Pro sports teach you the opposite, to be selfish, to worry about yourself and forget everyone else. We live in a bubble, filled with people telling us what we want to hear, and then when we retire, the bubble pops, and there's no one telling us how great we are any more. It sounds absurd, but that change can be crushing for some athletes. Their self-confidence takes a pounding, relationships suffer, and they make stupid decisions trying to get back that old feeling of being on top.

Regrettably, there are a lot of bad agents. Laziness plays a part, and there are also conflicts of interest. You have agents who have stakes in teams. It's against the rules, but it happens. Some of them will also make money advising teams on the market and what kind of riders are available. I don't know how an agent is supposed to represent me properly if he's also thinking about his own separate investments or contracts. Agents will also do group deals, where they'll bring four or five riders to the same team – essentially hoping to bargain with the group package. Either they want to tag a couple of guys onto the deal for a top rider, or they want to get a little bit more for themselves by doing it in bulk, because it's less work. That top rider might not realise it, but by being lazy, his agent is knocking a couple of hundred grand off his contract. That kind of conflict of interest is a huge concern when you've only got a few years in which to earn big money. I've also heard of agents being paid off by teams to drive prices down.

You're not always dealing with people who have high moral standards. If you look at a lot of agents, they're not actually qualified to do the job. There's nothing that says to me, 'This person has my best interests at heart.' They're not lawyers or accountants, or they don't have a business background, they've just found themselves in that position thanks to knowing the right people, because for all the changes we've seen in the last ten or twenty years, cycling is still a very secretive, close-knit little world. So you'll get someone who knows the sport a little, has some contacts, and he'll just sign up a few young riders and put himself in the middle of those deals. There are also good people out there with the right backgrounds, but the UCI's requirements aren't that stringent and I would say that they're not very well enforced, either. Unless you're representing a family member – for example, Alberto Contador's brother is his agent – you need to take a test, but it's not difficult.

I've seen teams employ people as advisors and then find out that they're also managing athletes privately, not on team contracts but on personal business, which is already a bit murky, and then I'll find out that the advisor has a brother who happens to be an agent, so the whole thing is as clear as mud. My agent once told me that he went to a meeting with one team, had the conversation, and then left to meet another team manager, only to find that the sports director from the previous meeting was there too because he was representing riders on the side. He was a former rider who had just retired and has since become a respected agent. He was obviously trying to decide between two careers paths at the time, and more than likely he was doing everything in an honest manner, but in a modern professional sport, there's no way that a person with a salaried position within a team should be advising athletes on their career choices. Even if they're totally irreproachable, the rules should protect us against that kind of behaviour.

Riders don't always see that side of the game, and maybe some don't care. There is no shortage of bad advice available to anyone willing to listen, and a lot of guys just have the wrong kind of people around them. They'll hear the sales pitch that sounds impressive, maybe the agent will get them lots of free stuff, and they'll think they're on to something good, but none of that matters. I changed representation during my career because when I met my current agent, I knew that he had the intelligence and the connections to do the best deals for me. I saw that he was able to create a market, and not just with three teams, with the whole field.

The sport is still very provincial. There are very few young French riders who'll end up riding for an Italian team, and that's because their market is in France and they're happy to stay close to home. It's not like football, where it's normal for a teenager to go abroad looking for opportunities. Just recently, Pietro Pellegri left the Italian Serie A team Genoa to play in France's Ligue 1 with AS Monaco, for a fee of around €25 million. He's one of Italy's brightest young stars, and he's only seventeen. I use him as an example, because the reality of his deal is that he's only moved a couple of hours down the coast, but in cycling you wouldn't see a neo-pro from Nice going the opposite direction to ride for an Italian squad. That's partly down to the fact that, as I said, cycling is still quite parochial, and it's also to do with the fact that it's in no one's interest to spend time and money on developing youth systems because in the current model, they get no money back if the rider leaves – there's no 'transfer fee'. I hope that cycling does more to cultivate young riders and I think we're starting to see it with some of the WorldTour teams that have development squads, but we're still decades behind the other major sports and I think we could do much more to incentivise that kind of long-term planning by teams.

I see cycling as being in a position similar to what football, or other league sports like baseball and American football, were in the 1970s and '80s. We still haven't figured out how to monetise it properly, how to share the revenues, how to promote growth. I hope that it's heading in the right direction, but as it is now I can't see it ever fulfilling its true potential. The best thing that could happen to cycling would be for one group to buy out everyone else and take total control. Now, you've got the ASO, who run the Tour de France and most of cycling's biggest one-day events, or RCS, who own the Giro d'Italia and all the Italian races, competing with each other over who has the biggest races and who can attract the best fields to their events, and the UCI looking on from the sidelines, trying to exert its own influence and make its own money. The teams operate within the UCI structure and they need the big race organisers because they own the events, but they're also a law unto themselves sometimes. Within the teams, you have interest groups, like Velon and the *Mouvement Pour un Cyclisme Crédible*, and they have their own agendas that don't always align with the preferences of the non-member teams, the UCI, or the race organisers. Everyone is pulling in different directions and it's a total mess. They're all trying to survive, and in doing so, they're just taking from one another rather than working together to find more resources.

It sucks when you see a team fold or a race get cancelled, even when it's nothing to do with you. I know from experience that it's demoralising when a sponsor pulls out and your team is forced to shut up shop. And, unfortunately, it's an experience that a lot of riders have to deal with at some point in their career. When it happened to me, I was in the car when I got the call. Actually, I got a call to warn me about the call. 'We're having a conference call in a few minutes, but it's not good news.'

We got lucky. The sponsor agreed to stay on for a while longer while the management found new backers, and the news never really got out to the wider public. Some people in cycling knew, but that was it. My results had been good the previous couple of seasons and I was young at the time, so I wasn't really that worried. For a guy like me, with some decent finishes at big races, there'll always be a team because the other managers start to circle like vultures the second they hear another team is in trouble, hoping to pick up the best riders at a discount. The people I really feel sorry for in those situations are the soigneurs and the mechanics. They're in a crowded market and it's not like they have the savings in the bank or the palmarès that a good rider can rely on to get him through the tough times. If the team collapses, they're in serious trouble.

There were similar problems on my first team. I'd signed a two-year contract when I turned pro, knowing that they only had a sponsor in place for the next twelve months. They managed to get one at the eleventh hour, but it was really close, almost the end of the year, before everything was 100 per cent secure. Again, because the shit only flirted with the fan rather than directly hitting it, their financial woes weren't public knowledge, and even if they were, they would have seemed commonplace to most seasoned observers. I don't think there's another sport in the world that has a more blasé approach to long-term economic stability.

THE 2018 GIRO D'ITALIA

Israel sucked. I didn't become a professional cyclist to fly somewhere to be stuck in a hotel. We were in Jerusalem, which is obviously really crowded, and no one was sure how easy it would be to get around with the bikes. We had to drive for an hour to get out of the city so that we could train for a couple of hours. We almost spent more time in the car than we did on our bikes. We'd leave at 9 a.m. and get back at 2 p.m. – all for a couple of hours riding on a highway in the middle of a desert. For me, cycling is about exploring and riding through interesting landscapes. It was also a nightmare logistically. The teams couldn't bring all the vehicles they'd usually have for a big race, so at the start of stage 2, in Haifa, you had fans and journalists walking around in the start village while we were trying to change our clothes in the cars. You might expect to see some bare arses like that at a really small continental race, but not at the Giro d'Italia.

I don't want to get into the politics too much, because everyone has their own views on the situation there and there are plenty of other people who could give you a more informed opinion on the pros and cons of running a sporting event in a troubled country.

From my perspective, I thought it was a little bit ironic to be asked about it so much by the media. There seemed to be plenty of journalists there who wanted to talk about Israel and Palestine – and some even openly criticised riders for not boycotting the race – while they were there too, expenses paid, enjoying the hospitality, trying to cause controversy. I'd understand that attitude if they had been political journalists, but they were the usual faces from the cycling media. Their TV channels, magazines and websites were all covering the race regardless. If they had a problem with the political situation, they should have boycotted the race themselves. Even if they just took a personal stand, their editor isn't going to fire them for it, but if a cyclist went to their team manager and said they couldn't do a race because of their political beliefs, I don't think he'd have a contract for too much longer.

It might not have been my first choice, but when you look at what football and the Olympics are doing, I don't think cycling is the only sport that needs a debate on this issue. I do have one clear memory of it being uncomfortable, though, when we passed by some fencing on the border. The road was lined with police vehicles and there were two helicopters overhead, but they weren't the TV helicopters that we're used to seeing. They were watching the Palestinians. It was a strange feeling.

At the time, I was more concerned about my race and all of the hoops we had to jump through. There were the problems with training in the build-up, and not having all of the team vehicles was a pain, but there were also little problems, like having to eat the hotel food because our chefs weren't allowed to use the kitchens there. There weren't even decent toilets at the start or finish, we were all using Portaloos. We joked about it, but it's crazy. 'Oh, you need a shit? There's a portable toilet over there, I hope you have plenty of hand sanitiser!' We spend all our time trying not to get sick, and then we're forced to deal with conditions like that. I can laugh about it now because it's so surreal, seeing a bunch of top professional athletes queueing up outside these plastic cabins before the prologue. And then on the 'rest day', which for the record might be one of the least appropriate names I can think of, we had to get up in the middle of the night to get to the airport to catch a four-hour chartered flight to Sicily. You don't mind that kind of transfer so much when it's back in Europe because there's the history and there are always so many fans. I think it's important for cycling to expand, but I don't know why we're going to places with no bike-racing culture. The races in the US or the UK are new too, but they sometimes get bigger crowds than you see on the Champs-Élysées for the Tour de France finale. And a short flight or a boat is OK. I flew to the start in 2017 too, because it was in Sardinia, but that's really short. When it's four hours, though, it has an effect on you. I felt fucked by the end of the first week, and the racing hadn't really even started. There were guys who had just finished the Tour de Romandie and gone home that Sunday night or Monday morning, only to fly out to Israel on Tuesday. They were trashed with all the travel before the Giro had even begun. It's not how you want to start one of the biggest races on the calendar.

After that flight from Israel, we arrived at the hotel in Sicily at around 1 p.m., had some lunch, and then had to go out for a training ride. And after three days there, we had to take a boat to the mainland after the Mount Etna stage. It was delayed, and I don't think we got to our hotel until about 10 p.m. or even later. So there were no massages, obviously. We just went to bed. Team Sky had a helicopter, which must have been nice. Some of the bunch thought that it was a bit ostentatious, and there was definitely some jealousy, but I couldn't understand why anyone would be pissed off at Team Sky for being more organised. It's different for the little Pro Continental teams that only made it into the Giro as wild cards, but all of the WorldTour teams have big budgets and I know for a fact that Sky weren't the only outfit to be given a financial incentive by the organisers beforehand. If those tired, green-eyed riders shuffling onto the ferry wanted to be annoyed at anyone, they should have looked closer to home. That helicopter was on the list of optional extras that the teams were offered by RCS before the start. It cost €5,000. Not a large sum, in the grand scheme of things, but some of the team managers are so cheap that they wouldn't spend at Christmas. And they don't seem interested in any revenue stream other than sponsorships. For one, I don't understand why they don't have merchandise trucks at the big races. It's crazy. All those fans, and they don't even try to sell them anything. And then they complain about budgets. I know guys in the bunch who make thousands a month selling their own merchandise, so what would a team make? They have a bigger reach, a whole squad of guys with their own fans, some big stars, Grand Tour winners or Classics guys, world champions, whatever. You'd have to think that they could make some money from that. No one even bothers. And when they're offered a helicopter for their tired and hungry riders, €5,000 is too pricey. I wish they'd sell some fucking T-shirts and some caps and get us to the hotel quicker. I don't think it's that difficult. Most of the time, not even the sponsors try that. Before the Tour in 2018, Hansgrohe genuinely went viral by releasing a limited-edition Peter Sagan shower head. It was silly, but it worked, it was all over the media. Just a fun little story, nothing serious or hard to do, but everyone was reading about Hansgrohe. And who knew what they did before that? That was smart marketing.

Anyway, back to the Giro. The route was a good one, on the whole.

Stage 10 was a surprise, because I hadn't expected it to be so hard. I think it was the hardest of the whole race. It was the longest stage, but in theory it didn't look so tough. It was lumpy but there weren't any massive climbs. In practice, it was 244 kilometres on the limit. It probably didn't seem that way to fans watching at home, because the TV helicopters only started broadcasting after 100 kilometres, I think. So we'd already been riding on the limit for two hours. There was a breakaway right from the start, so the bunch was pulling to catch them, but then when word got around that Esteban Chaves had cracked, the pace increased because the general classification guys wanted to finish him off. There's always someone who collapses like that after the rest days. It's not nice to see, especially because Chaves seems like a nice guy and he's worked really hard to get back to his best after a difficult 2017, but that's bike racing. He looked to be in top shape when he won on Mount Etna, but he was lacking stamina. It goes to show that you never know in a Grand Tour.

The next couple of stages were more of the same. We'd expected them to be fairly chilled in the build-up to two important mountain stages – first to Monte Zoncolan and then the next day too – but we raced like maniacs for the whole week. I'm sure it was exciting on television, I just wish I'd been on my couch enjoying it with everyone else.

Zoncolan was incredible. It's a crazy climb, really steep and tight, almost claustrophobic, and because of the landscape and the way the crowds completely surround you, riding into it feels like a stadium, but I'd done my work for the day when it got to the hardest part so I could just take it easy. I was actually joking with the fans, yelling 'Spingi, spingi! Push, push!' When Froome won, it was a great way for him to win his first-ever stage at the Giro, but I still thought that he was just hunting for stages. I didn't think he had any chance of winning it. Even the next day, he lost a minute and a half to Yates. It looked like he was totally out of contention.

For some reason, the evening after stage 19 stands out as a nightmare. We had dinner at around nine o'clock, and went up to bed an hour later, but you still need time there to chill out and decompress – it's not like you can just lie down and sleep right away. You're in the middle of a huge race, there's always so many things on your mind, and on top of that, you're full of aches and pains and in a new environment. The hotels aren't always the best, so you could be trying to deal with a crappy bed or someone outside the room making lots of noise. And as I'm sure a lot of amateurs will know, sometimes after a big day on the bike, you can almost be too tired to sleep. But at 7 a.m., it's breakfast, and you have to be ready to do it all again. The departure to the start in Susa was 8 a.m., and then we had a long drive from the finish in Cervinia to the hotel, but we had to be ready to go to the airport almost right away, with our hand-luggage and our passports. I think we got to the hotel in Rome at about midnight – and that was after a 214-kilometre mountain stage. Six hours on the bike and then all that bullshit, but that's the norm. And the final stage in Rome was an absolute disgrace. The city government there had signed a multi-year deal with the Giro organisers to bring the race to Rome and then they didn't bother to make even basic repairs to the roads. I'd heard they were bad, but I wasn't expecting anything like what we found, they were unusable. A few of the big-name GC riders like Tom Dumoulin deserve a lot of credit for going to the organisers and neutralising the race. Technically, they could have kept the pressure up and hoped that Sky and Chris Froome would crash out of the race, but no one wants to win like that. You don't battle each other for thousands of kilometres only to let a few shitty potholes decide the outcome. It was a shame to see the GC guys finish so far behind the sprint, but that's what you get when you organise a shambles like that. I can understand why they'd want to bring us through the historical centre and past all the nice buildings because it looked incredible on television, but the roads were not fit for racing. I don't even think I'd like to drive my car on them. If everyone had been going full gas, it would have been carnage, crashes and flat tyres everywhere, and that's not what anyone deserves after three weeks of proper Grand Tour racing.

A lot of people underestimate the effect that the travel between stages can have on us. Even my family and friends don't quite get it; sometimes I'll talk to someone after a stage, and they'll ask, 'Did you have dinner?' or something like that, because they're thinking about their own day. But for us, the stage finished, then there are interviews, the bus ride back to the hotel, showers and massages ... We'll eat something on the bus, but for us it's more like lunch at 6 p.m.; dinner is rarely before nine. If a stage finishes around 5.30 or 6 p.m., we might not be in the hotel for another two hours, and then it'll take the soigneurs a couple of hours to get through all of the massages. Apart from those big mountain stages, the mornings are easier. We'll eat three hours before the stage, so usually when I wake up there's time to relax in my room for a bit, and I'll make my own coffee and do some stretching before a late breakfast. If there has to be a transfer, I'd prefer it in the morning. You have to eat a lot a few hours before the race anyway, so you're up early for that and to pack your case so that the team can put it in the truck. After that, it doesn't make much difference to me whether I'm chilling out in the bus or back in my room. When it comes after the stage, you're tired and uncomfortable, and it pushes the schedule on too much. You're late getting a massage or maybe you have to skip it, you're late eating dinner, and you're late to bed. And meanwhile, you still need to upload your data for the team and fill in your log book. That's before you talk to your family.

There's not a lot we can do about that stuff – it's what makes a Grand Tour a Grand Tour. You have to travel the whole country, and now I think that the foreign starts are just part of it all. Some people might not like them, but the organisers are in this business to make money, and especially during the recession I don't think it was always easy to find money close to home. As well as that, I think it's cool that fans everywhere can see the best riders in an important race. When you think of the crowds that the Tour or the Giro got in recent years when they went to the UK, to Ireland, or the Netherlands, it was special. It's a pain in the arse for everyone involved, but on the whole it's worth it.

I think a lot of people look back to the old days and assume that the racing was harder. For sure, the equipment today makes a big difference and the teams and race organisers take better care of us in terms of safety, nutrition, medical attention, all of that. But they didn't have any team buses, so they didn't do many transfers. Most of the time, they just finished in a town one day and started there the next, so there was more down time and logistically it was a lot simpler.

As for the stars of the race, Simon Yates was amazing. But that shows you why a Grand Tour has to be three weeks long. There's always talk about shortening them, the Giro and the Vuelta a España especially, but this is what makes them so difficult. It's a war of attrition, it's not just about being strong for a few days or a week. If that Giro had been two weeks, it would have been Simon's, he was by far the strongest. Up until stage 15, he'd won three stages and he had more than two minutes on guys like Tom Dumoulin, Domenico Pozzovivo, and Thibaut Pinot. And almost five minutes on Chris Froome. Even after stage 18, he still had almost half a minute on Dumoulin – that's more or less the margin by which the Dutchman had won the year before. All the talk on the second rest day was that Yates was going to win it easily. He was totally in charge, until he wasn't.

When you crack, you crack. There's no coming back from it. It's different when you have a crash or a mechanical that costs you time: if you're still in good shape you can work your way back up the classification, especially at a Grand Tour because they're so long and you can almost bet on someone else having problems. But when your body gives up, there's nothing you can do. Every racer has been there. It happens to the best of us. I've dropped right out of races in what felt like the blink of an eye. One minute you're fine, and then you're just totally empty.

Look at what happened to Thibaut Pinot. He was third on stage 19, and then he lost almost forty-four minutes the next day and had to retire from the race. He was so bad when he got back to the team hotel that they called an ambulance and he ended up getting treatment in hospital for severe dehydration and fever. To me, that looks like a big problem with his nutritional programme. It's one of the hardest things to get right at a Grand Tour. On the big stages, you might burn through 6,000 calories, and you need to eat maybe 9,000 to recover. Even if you manage 7,000 calories, that's still 2,000 short, that's almost what a normal guy eats in a day. Just getting all of it into you is a problem, even with things like recovery shakes. Pinot put in a huge effort on the final climb of stage 19 trying to limit the losses to Froome and make up some ground and he ended up paying for it dearly. That's something you learn with experience. I had a feeling that his race was finished after Bardonecchia.

It's hard to blame anyone for that. The team could have taken better care of him, perhaps, but I wasn't there to see so I don't know. It's also possible that he's just not cut out for three weeks of racing. There are plenty of riders who have the potential on paper, but real life is a different thing. It takes a special kind of physiology, and it's rare. That's why there are thirty or forty guys who can win a Grand Tour stage and only five or six who can win the general classification. Pinot is reaching the age now where he should have figured himself out. I think that Giro was his tenth Grand Tour. He's still only twenty-eight and he's got lots of talent, at least going uphill, but youth can't be an excuse any more. Having said that, the way he finished 2018, winning Milano–Torino and then Il Lombardia, he has to be hopeful about the next couple of seasons. You don't win a Monument like that unless you've got something special.

Simon Yates is different. He's twenty-six, and he's still learning his craft. I also think he came really close at the Giro, and if the racing hadn't been so hard he could have held on. In the days leading up to his collapse, I'm sure his team knew it was coming, but in a situation like that you're just praying for an easy day and some kind of recovery. It must have been a huge disappointment to lose the maglia rosa, but he got some brilliant stage victories and must have learned a whole lot of invaluable lessons because he came back and won a great Vuelta later in the season. His talent has been obvious for a long time, but that kind of reaction shows that he has the right mentality, too. There's a thin line between winning and losing at a Grand Tour, and sometimes you just have to do the latter before the former is possible. You encounter problems that you could never fully appreciate until you're in that situation, and there's always a certain amount of trial and error involved in development. He would have left the Giro disappointed, but excited about the fact that he'd proved he was good enough to beat the best at one of cycling's most important events. And he didn't second-guess himself the next time an opportunity arose. He got acclimatised to life at the top, and all the added pressures that involves: the extra press conferences, the extra doping controls, the media scrutiny, all the eyes in the bunch watching you constantly. There's a good reason why the best riders don't want to take a jersey too early – it can be exhausting. Also, regarding his preparation, he took a big break before the Giro, and hadn't raced since March, when he did the Volta a Catalunya, so that's something to think about. He was in better shape going into the Vuelta, despite having already given 100 per cent at a Grand Tour. Perhaps more racing leading into his next Giro attempt will help him.

Was Froome a surprise? It can't really be shocking with a guy who has a palmarès like that. And we know how quickly a Giro can turn – just look at Vincenzo Nibali in 2016. All I can say is that Froome must have really big balls to start a Grand Tour the way he did and gamble on coming good in the third week. There was no Nibali or Nairo Quintana, but it was a really strong field. When I saw him in the bunch during the first week, he didn't make much of an impression at all. He seemed so relaxed, chatting away, he was also talking a lot on the mic back to the directors, and I passed him a couple of times, thinking, 'You need to pedal more and talk less, because you're losing time here.'

It could have been the plan, to take some of the attention away from him. There was all the controversy about his salbu-tamol case and whether or not he should have been racing, and there was talk about a Giro-Tour double. That's a lot for anyone to handle. The fact that Yates did so well early on, coupled with Dumoulin being the defending champion and looking so strong, that must have helped him. A five-time Grand Tour champion is never going to fly under the radar, but it definitely wasn't the Chris Froome show that everyone's used to.

Regardless of how you feel about him, you have to admire anyone who can execute a solo attack like that for 80 kilometres. Just look at what he did on stage 19. That was crazy. It was a breath-taking spectacle in terms of the physical requirement, but more than that, it must have taken nerves of steel. Mess that up, and you'd be ridiculed, especially when you've won as much as he has. He just never quits. It was funny to see him running up Mont Ventoux in 2016 when his bike broke and it's easy to make jokes about how dumb it looked or about the fact that he should have known that it was against the rules, but on the serious side, that's a real competitor. He never gives up. I expected him to try his luck on the Colle delle Finestre, but I thought he'd go with some teammates and try and do a team time trial to the finish, but I never thought he'd go alone.

Even at the top of the Finestre, he had around thirty-eight seconds, and I thought that was nothing. The other leaders were chasing him – Dumoulin, Pinot, Miguel Ángel López and Richard Carapaz – and even allowing for the fact that Pinot is a poor descender, I thought they'd pull him along and then work together to catch Froome. Perhaps the other teams could have performed better tactically, but it's impossible to plan for a huge gamble like that. The two South Americans might have worked together and contested for the stage win, or Team Sunweb and Groupama–FDJ could have tried to do a deal with the other teams to work together, but in the heat of the moment, with the pressure of racing, making split-second decisions, and also with the language barriers, it's not easy. When I got to see the replay, it looked like everyone else was just relying on Dumoulin to do all the work, which is a shame because a forty-second gap really isn't a lot when it's four against one, going full gas. Who knows, maybe Team Sky made a deal with them. That kind of thing doesn't go on as often as it used to, but it can happen. Anyway, the way Froome descended on the Finestre was astonishing. That's where he won the whole race. It's funny to think that a few years ago, people made fun of him on the downhills. In all my years of racing, it was one of the most spectacular things I've seen and when someone has the guts to risk it all like that, then you have to applaud them.

THE 2018 TOUR DE FRANCE

At the start of the year, I didn't even think I was riding the Tour de France. I was planning a nice holiday, and maybe some media work. I probably would have made more money not doing the Tour than doing it, but as the season progressed I had a feeling that I'd be asked to go. The 2018 Tour was a good one, if you ask me. There were some riders complaining about the cobbles on the stage to Roubaix, but that's a part of cycling. It's not just about being the fastest rider uphill or the fastest rider in theory, it isn't a computer game. If you want to win a Grand Tour, you need to be good at it all, and bike-handling on difficult surfaces is a part of that. If I was a kid watching that stage at home, I'd have been glued to the television. It's not like they're throwing in three or four stages like that every year, but one cobbled day every year or every second year seems like a good idea to me.

It was hard to understand the complaints. They said it was dangerous, but it's only dangerous if you're a bad bike handler. And anyway, danger and risk are aspects of cycling. Would anyone tune in if we were all just racing on stationary bikes in a gym somewhere? I don't think so.

If it were up to me, I'd have scheduled the cobbles after some hard mountain stages. Geographically that's a challenge because they're not near any of the mountains, but I'd try to work something out. The racing is always more dangerous when the general classification hasn't been established, and there were a lot of nervous riders trying to get to the front because no one wanted to lose time so early. I actually like to see mountain stages in the first week of Grand Tours, because it calms everything down a little bit. When it's just a week of flat stages for sprinters, the stress in the bunch is crazy. And if the cobbles came towards the middle of the race, someone like Richie Porte, who doesn't like that kind of riding, would be more likely to play it safe on the pavé because he might have had a decent result in the mountains and built up some time. It might not sound like a big difference to fans, but the hardest part about that stage was the fact that everyone was so anxious about crashing out before the race had even got to the mountains. Richie crashed and had to retire because of a collarbone fracture, and that was his whole season messed up. You'd still be pissed off if you crashed out in the second week, but it's not as depressing if you've already won a big stage.

It's hard not to feel sorry for a guy like that when they crash out, but that's bike racing. It's not like the organisers were personally out to get him. And he knew that the stage was coming for almost a year, it wasn't a surprise. If you're not comfortable with an aspect of racing, whether it's cobbles or time trialling or descending, the only solution is to practise. A DS from one of the teams actually joked with me at the finish one day that rather than feeling sorry for Richie, we should feel sorry for the teams who keep giving him big contracts, because every time he races a Grand Tour there seems to be some big problem. That's harsh, but it might be fair too. They're paying him millions and he never delivers. Regardless of whether you're a Chris Froome fan or not, the man always delivers somehow. He's not in that pile-up, or he doesn't get sick, or have a bad day in the mountains that ends up costing him ten minutes. Porte was an incredible super-domestique at Sky for Brad Wiggins and Froome, but leading a team is a different challenge entirely. Once or twice is bad luck, but if it happens time and again, there's something

THE 2018 TOUR DE FRANCE

missing with the rider. It could be day-dreaming or not taking enough care of yourself, but there's something not right. I'm no different. I've had crashes that were totally out of my hands, but if I'm being honest with myself, there were also a few that I could, and should, have avoided. In contrast to that, it was a shame to see Vincenzo Nibali leaving the race because of one idiotic fan and his camera strap, but there's nothing you can do about that, short of erecting thirty kilometres of barriers. Some of those fans almost look like they're playing chicken with the riders, waiting until the last second before jumping out of the way.

It was nice to see John Degenkolb win again, after that car crashed into him and his teammates during a training camp in 2016. He seems like a good guy, and he had been incredible the year before, winning both Milano–Sanremo and Paris–Roubaix. I don't think anyone had done that since Sean Kelly in the 1980s. A lot of people were wondering if he'd come back from that because it didn't seem like he was the same after his recovery, but winning in Roubaix at the Tour de France put an end to that speculation.

Greg Van Avermaet was impressive. When he went in that break in the mountains on stage 10, that was cool. A lot of people seemed surprised by him, but it wasn't a shock to me. He's a world-class rider, and he'd looked really impressive at the Tour de Suisse. You have to remember too that he won an intermediate mountains stage at the Tour back in 2015, and he would have won the Clásica de San Sebastián that year too if that TV motorbike hadn't hit him on the final climb. And when he won his Olympic gold in 2016 in Brazil, that was a climber's parcours. He's best known as a Classics specialist, obviously, but the guy is no slouch uphill either.

I don't know what Movistar were trying to do with Mikel Landa, Alejandro Valverde, and Nairo Quintana. That's too many leaders to juggle if you ask me. All of them seem like good professionals, but they're also all big talents, they all want to win, and I don't know how anyone expects to manage that at a Grand Tour. You might get them to agree to work together before the race, but they all have egos, and that's not a bad thing. You need ego to compete at that level, so it's not like Landa is going to be happy working as a domestique.

With the Mûr-de-Bretagne and the cobbles, it was a parcours for good racers. Before the start I fancied Vincenzo Nibali or Tom Dumoulin because I think they're the best all-rounders. These days you'd have to say that Froome is a good racer now too, even though he still looks like dogshit on the bike, spinning away, all elbows and knees, staring at his computer. He's fast, but he is not nice to watch. I wouldn't care how I looked if I was winning all those races though.

What Geraint Thomas achieved was a huge surprise to me. I never believed that he could win a Tour. He'd never even managed a top ten before. I don't know what changed. He was always a good rider, he's won some good road races and you certainly don't win all those Olympic medals without a special talent, but a three-week Grand Tour is a different animal. Maybe if Nibali had still been in the race it would have been a different outcome, but I don't think anyone should dismiss Thomas's win by saying that it was made easier by the fact that Dumoulin and Chris Froome had been at the Giro. I saw those guys up close, they were in great shape. Look at how both of them rode the time trial on the penultimate day – they were first and second, fourteen or fifteen seconds faster than Thomas. They're both brilliant at the TT, but even with all the talent in the world it's impossible to put in that kind of performance when you're tired. I can see why it seemed a bit cold of Team Sky to not back Thomas sooner, but from their point of view, Froome is the man. He always delivers. Since 2013, he's been on the podium of every Grand Tour he finished, and he won six of them. If you're betting on anyone, it's going to be him.

The fact that in 2018 new rules meant all the teams had one less rider didn't make too much of a difference, in my opinion. The big squads found it harder to bet on two horses – a sprinter and a general classification man – but other than that, it was the same. The richest teams still have the best rosters, taking away one rider doesn't change that because it's something that affects all of the teams equally. It made a bigger difference at the Classics because I think it was harder for the big teams to really control the race, and they had fewer riders to gamble with when it came to attacks. Team Sky went to the Tour with Froome, Geraint Thomas, Wout Poels and Michał Kwiatkowski. They're all potential leaders at a WorldTour team. The wage bill alone at Sky is supposedly around €27 million – that's more than double the entire budget of most other teams. The small continental teams like Wanty–Groupe Gobert who get invited as wildcards are probably operating on less than Froome alone gets paid.

Reducing the team size does make a difference, but maybe the impact is not enough. It's harder to control the bunch, but I think for it to make a real impact on a big team, they would need to lose a couple of riders. If teams were still going to the Grand Tours with a sprinter and a climber or a GC rider, it would be a lot harder for the teams to manage and the domestiques would need to work even harder than they already do, but no one seems to be doing that. By just choosing to go with one objective – concentrating on the sprints, mountain stage wins or the GC – they've nullified the effect that the change was supposed to have. And maybe that actually gives an advantage to the big stars, because they don't have to share the team with anyone. All of those guys at Sky were there with one goal:

win the general classification. You could feel it more in the Classics though, it was harder for a team like Quick-Step Floors to really dominate. But they didn't do too badly anyway – they still won two Monuments. I'm still not certain that taking away a rider from each team isn't really going to impact the racing. Earlier in the season it looked like it was having an effect, but the Tour was different. The only way that the UCI could make a big difference to how we race is to limit the financial side somehow, because the richest teams have the deepest squads and the biggest stars.

I'm not so sold on the short mountain stages either, but that's probably a personal bias. I prefer the long stages because I'm more of a diesel, and that's the cycling I grew up with. I hope the race organisers don't go too far that way, but I can understand the appeal of it, and again, if I was a kid watching at home, I'd have loved it because there's the potential for action from start to finish. It's good to see that they're willing to try new things, the sport has to evolve, and there are other guys in the peloton who love that kind of racing. Once it's a good mix, it's a positive thing. Cycling is an endurance sport, so we need those 220-kilometre stages in the mountains, but there's no harm in a couple of short days either if it makes the race more enticing. As for the grid start which has been suggested, I think the jury is still out. Again, it's worth trying new things, but nothing happened and compared to motor-sports, cyclists are a bit slower to take off, so it wasn't much of a spectacle.

Unfortunately, there were a couple of spectacles that the sport could have done without. I don't really know Gianni Moscon. He could be a great guy away from racing, but on the bike it seems like he has some serious issues. As far as I'm concerned, he got off extremely lightly in 2017, when he racially abused French cyclist Kevin Reza at the Tour de

Romandie. In the heat of the moment it's easy to lose your head, but not like that. That's something inside of him. Call him a dickhead or tell him to fuck off, that's fine, but there's no excuse for racism. It's the twenty-first century, for Christ's sake. He just got off with a slap on the wrist – a six-week suspension and a warning from the team – and a few months later he was back in trouble for when Sébastien Reichenbach accused him of knocking him off his bike at a race in Italy. He wasn't punished because there was no video evidence, but his reputation has suffered. That's two serious incidents, which is two more chances than he should have needed to figure out that he can't be an ignorant bully if he wants to be a professional cyclist. Rather than learn his lesson though, he goes and punches Élie Gesbert at the Tour, and what did Sky do? Nothing. They said after Romandie that his contract would be terminated if he messed up again, but they didn't have the balls to fire him because they know he's talented. Or maybe they just don't really care. Either way, it sets a shitty example. They made excuses for him, put it down to his age, but he's twenty-four now, some riders are already winning massive races at that age. And anyway, it's not like he's some neo-pro at a small continental team. He's riding for the biggest outfit in professional cycling. If he's old enough to ride with the best in the world, he's old enough to behave himself.

And then came the tear gas. I didn't know what was going on. It was early in the day, about 25 kilometres from the start of stage 16 in Carcassonne, and we were taking it easy. As I rolled up I could see the road was blocked with bales of hay and then all of a sudden, my eyes started burning. The farmers were protesting against some kind of cut in state aid and things must have got heated because the police decided to spray them with tear gas. Who knows what they were thinking. In general,

I think that's a pretty crazy reaction to some tractors and hay bales, but in the middle of the biggest bike race on the planet? It was surreal, Geraint Thomas in the yellow jersey and Peter Sagan in the green jersey, rubbing their eyes like crazy, with the race doctors rushing around with water and eye drops. And this is being broadcast around the world. Well done, guys. It's the kind of thing that could only happen in cycling. Imagine Lionel Messi on the sidelines of a Champions League game, grasping for a bottle of eye drops. When you go to a race like the Tour, you have to be ready for anything, but that's taking the piss.

CRASHES

It only takes a second to undo hundreds of hours training and thousands of kilometres hard work. It could be a lapse of concentration, someone else's mistake … or even some shit equipment you've been forced to use. It could just be a gust of wind. Wrong place, wrong time, and bang, your season is over, maybe your career, or worse. It's a sickening feeling, the grim inevitability of knowing that sooner or later, you're going to fall.

And it's not just the crash. The crash sucks, but it's what comes after that makes it so much worse. You can have a fall at the start of a Grand Tour and it might not be so bad, some bruising and a little road rash, but because you're racing every day you're constantly changing the dressing and being careful of the wounds. And if it's something worse than just a gash? It's a nightmare, every morning waking up to pain and dirty bandages, and with bruised or broken bones it makes it incredibly hard to do simple tasks. Not what you want before a 250-kilometre-long stage, when all you should be worrying about is eating enough and trying to get a decent coffee.

Being sent home is even worse. A broken pelvis is horrific. And then you're lying around the house with everyone looking at you, that's not great when you have kids because they don't want to see Daddy looking like he's been in a world championship boxing match. It sucks for the rider too. That shouldn't be forgotten. There's a lot of bravado in cycling, especially among the amateurs, about how hard it is, about all of the suffering, but after so many years of having to deal with it, you can keep your suffering. Crashes and pain don't make you a better cyclist, they just make you an uncomfortable one.

Whether you're a neo-pro or an old hand, a domestique or a multiple Grand Tour winner, it's all the same: the first goal at every race is to stay on your bike. It sounds obvious but it's true. I know one guy whose agent will call him up before a big race for a pep talk, and then sign off the call by yelling, 'Don't fucking crash!' That's a little too on the nose for some people, but it's still solid advice. Whatever job you have to do in the race, you're not going to do it on the floor, and regardless of whether your DS wants you to act as a mule, going back and forth from the car to the front with food and water bottles, or if you're there to contend for the victory, it's going to be a lot easier if you stay out of trouble.

Tunnels can be a bit of a problem, psychologically at least. I've never seen a crash in a tunnel, it's just a feeling. It always feels like a massive tailwind in a tunnel. It must be the force of the group and all the cars coming into it, but there always seems to be a big gust behind us. If you watch, we'll always go faster in tunnels. It's also a problem if you're at the back of the bunch, where you'd normally have a nice draft, because when you ride in there you have to sprint for your life just to hang on, it's like the front guys are being sucked out the front. We call it 'the tunnel effect'. I can remember a couple of times at the Vuelta a Catalunya, coming out of Andorra to Spain, there are lots of tunnels, and they've helped the peloton catch the breakaways. And my friends who've done the Tour of Turkey told me that the Eurasia tunnel is frightening. It goes underneath the Bosphorus strait and they pass through it at 100km/h. Scary. In the lead-up to something like that, I'll just try to get my glasses off. A lot of guys will also close an eye a few hundred metres beforehand, because when you open it again you're more adjusted to the darkness. But sometimes you can't do anything to prepare yourself. At the Giro in 2018, with five kilometres to go to the finish, there was a tunnel with no lights. And in their infinite wisdom, the organisation decided to put flares in there. It was just before a bunch sprint, with a couple of big corners to come, and we were all half-blind, with smoke in our eyes. That was terrifying. It was like riding into hell, all we could see was red smoke. And no one thought, 'Isn't clean air important to cyclists?'

Crashing is not something that any rider wants to be known for, but like most veterans, I've had a few beauties over the years. I've broken more bones than I could name, lost a lot of skin. I'm surprised that I still have all my teeth. Some injuries are more annoying than others though because there's just no getting away from the pain. Road rash isn't as serious as a fractured skull, for instance, but it can quite literally be a huge pain in the arse if you can't sit down properly. Shoulder and arm injuries really suck too because you can't do simple things like make a coffee or eat your food without someone helping you.

When you crash, you can't see yourself go down, and with all the adrenalin pumping, you rarely realise how bad it is. Sometimes, it's too much. In hindsight I've kept going a couple of times when I shouldn't have. As one director said to me on the roadside after a bad pile-up, while we were arguing about me getting back on my bike, 'It's a bike race, not a fucking circus.'

The compulsion is just to get back on the bike and keep racing. It would have to be something like a broken limb or a damaged pelvis to stop me. If I can still push the pedals, I'm going to keep riding. I don't remember much about my worst accidents, or at least, I don't remember much about them first hand. After the race, when I'm home and I can watch the replays, you obviously remember it all happening, but your frame of mind is totally different in the moment, you're just panicking about losing too much time, anxious to get going again. The desire to win is incredibly strong in cycling, but none of the management team I work with would ever risk a rider's safety. With all my big crashes, the sports directors have always told me to stop, to just get into the ambulance and call it a day. If I've continued, it was my call. They don't want you to hurt yourself, but everyone knows how hard it is to just give up when you've worked all year for something. Our careers are so short, and to race a Grand Tour or a Monument is such a privilege, you never want to waste that opportunity. Team allegiances usually get put aside when someone has had a bad fall, we've all been there and no one wants to see you go home like that. We want to win, but on the bike. I've been pushed to the finish line in one race by a world champion. He didn't have to do it, we weren't teammates, but to see someone in the rainbow jersey make that effort, it's a gesture I'll never forget.

One of the worst-looking accidents I can remember was when the Dutch rider Laurens ten Dam crashed at the 2011 Tour de France. He cut his face up really bad, and had to ride on with a makeshift, bloodied bandage wrapped around his face. It might have looked worse than it actually was, but as a bystander, it was fairly gruesome. He was determined to go on though, and in the days after, I remember hearing him joke with some of the guys in the bunch that when he met his wife at the finish line, she'd told him to suck it up because you don't leave the Tour de France because of a split lip.

We're able to laugh about that stuff because it's a part of what we do, but I don't like it when it's glamorised by the media or the fans. I can think of a few times I've crashed when it's been totally my own fault, I've just looked around or switched off at the worst possible moment, going into a tough corner with too much speed or with the totally wrong line, and afterwards I'll be furious with myself because it's such an avoidable mistake. If you crash because of a mechanical issue, or because someone else goes down and takes you with them, that's one thing, it's just an inescapable part of bike racing and there's no point losing sleep over it. But when you do it to yourself, it's exasperating. I've been in this game long enough to know how to go around a corner properly. So it's irritating to hear people talking about it like it's cool. It might be cool that I didn't make a big deal about it and managed to stay in the race, but I think it would be a lot cooler to not have fallen off my bike in the first place. People will pat you on the back like you're a hero, and I can see why they like it – compared to other sports, we can seem like hard men – but in your own head, all you can think is that you were a stupid fucker for missing the corner.

The good thing about most cyclists is that we forget these things quickly. I don't want to make it sound like we're simpletons because I know quite a few guys in the bunch who are very intelligent, lots of them are studying or running successful businesses on the side, but when it comes to our day jobs, it's better not to be a deep thinker. It's been a few months now since I've crashed and the short-term memory is already fading. I know it sucks because it's happened so many times, but I'm already convincing myself that it wasn't that bad. When it happens again though, it'll all come flooding back, and I'll say to myself, 'Wrong again, this fucking hurts, man.' And I'm old now too, so the bones are less forgiving than they used to be.

Usually it happens when you're tired, or trying to ride yourself into shape at a stage race. You'll be pushing yourself too hard, hanging on for dear life, just trying to make it to the top of a climb without being dropped, and by the time you reach the peak, you're cooked. It's hard to concentrate, you're trying to recover, but you still have to keep pushing, and the pace can be terrifying, especially when you're out of sorts. If you're really bad, it can be disorientating, and you're going into corners without really knowing for sure what you're doing. Your line will be all over the place, your mind distracted. And you can never react quick enough. You can see it coming, but you know it's too late, there are a few seconds filled with dread as you brace yourself for the grim inevitability of what's to come – pain, and lots of it. For some guys, the first thought after impact might be for their family back home watching or worrying about the damage they might have done, and I get that, it's not nice for the wife and kids to see you like that, but it's not nice for yourself, either. I have to say that for me, it's always the same thought: continuing. It's all I can think about. I never want a DNF by my name, especially not at a big race like the Giro or the Tour. I'll be desperately looking around for the race doctor, praying that he can fix me up and get me going again.

That's why I'm always telling the young guys: recon rides are so important, you need to pay close attention. If you've done a Classic four or five times, for example, you'll generally know the danger spots, but with something like Il Lombardia, they're always messing around with the course, so it's still useful to ride it beforehand. In 2017, Quick-Step Floors' Laurens De Plus had a horrific crash at that race descending the Muro di Sormano. I knew the bend well, so I took it easy, but he was trying to catch the AG2R La Mondiale rider Mikel Cherel. He totally misjudged the bend and hit the guard rail, which fired him into the air and over the edge.

There's no such thing as a fortunate crash, because if he had luck on his side he wouldn't have hit the rail in the first place, but it could have been a lot worse. Some of the verges on that road are incredibly steep, almost vertical, and when you see it first on TV, it genuinely looks like he's just gone off a cliff. It was a relief to see him caught up in some trees and bushes not too far below the road. It was worse for another Belgian, Jan Bakelants, who crashed on the same corner but ended up falling deeper into the ravine. He ended up in intensive care with broken ribs and fractured vertebrae. Someone posted a photograph of his bicycle three or four metres above where he landed, stuck in the branches. A young Italian rider by the name of Simone Petilli fell there too, and was diagnosed with a fracture in his neck that could have been fatal if not discovered. And that's just one bend at one race – you could fill a book with stories of gnarly crashes each and every season.

Every time something like that happens, someone starts talking about the descents being too dangerous or about race organisers not caring about the riders, but I just think it's a part of the sport, and if you want to include the Muro di Sormano in the race, you have to descend that side, there's no option. It's a brutal climb, and an iconic one, so if I was the organiser, I'd want to include it. Before the race, it gets people talking and generates more interest, and during the race it gives the most explosive riders an opportunity to do something special. I wouldn't sacrifice all of that just because the other side of it is technically difficult and potentially dangerous. If you get rid of the speed and the danger, there's not a lot left. Despite my previous protestations, our equipment is better than it's ever been, and no one is forcing you to go that fast. On a long climb, we have to manage our efforts because if you went as fast as possible you'd be cooked in no time, and I think it's the same with descending. It's not about going as fast as humanly possible, it's about going as fast as your personal ability allows. I'm a good descender, but I'm not going to try to beat Peter Sagan down a mountain. It's just racing, and it's up to us to go slower if we're worried about a descent. Even an uncomplicated, mellow downhill can be made dangerous if a rider wants to take serious risks. For proof of that, just look at the way Marco Pantani used to descend. It was a peculiar technique that he perfected at an early age to get as aerodynamic as possible, but if the average cyclist started hanging their weight out over the back wheel like that, with the saddle pressed into their chest, it wouldn't be too long before they had a serious accident. Some of the guys in the bunch now like to get down on the crossbar, tucked in behind the handlebars, and if you're good at it and have a lot of bike-handling skills, it is faster, but it's also a lot more precarious.

Don't get me wrong when I say that it's just a part of the job. It is, but it's a part of the job that really sucks. No one wants to see a crash happen, least of all a guy like me, who has experienced it more times than I'd care to remember. The organisers can always do more to make the route as safe as possible, and it's definitely improved in my time, but there's a limit to what's feasible. We could have had nets on that corner, like they have in skiing, but it could just as easily have been another bend. You can't put padding, nets, and hay bales on every corner of a 250-kilometre race course. The nature of bike racing is that it's unpredictable and the worst things can happen at any moment. A great example of that was the 2014 Tour de France, when half of the bunch were shitting themselves before stage 5 from Ypres to Arenberg Porte du Hinaut, because the parcours included nine sections of the horrible cobbles that feature in Paris–Roubaix cycle. And in the end, Chris Froome crashed twice on the normal roads and was forced out of the race with fractures in his hands. You couldn't have predicted that. Plenty of people would have put money on one of the general classification favourites crashing on the pavé, but not on some random flat road.

Some races are better than others when it comes to alerting you to the dangers, and I think that's a better strategy for avoiding really bad crashes than putting up nets and padding. The Tour de Suisse started using signposted arrows a few years back to warn you of things like hairpin bends, and that's helpful because if you happen to have switched off for a second, which can happen over the course of a long day, it snaps you back into it in time to stay out of trouble.

It also helps to be in a good position in the bunch before the technical stuff, and if you're in a small group, it's important to make sure you're with the right guys because it's surprising how bad some riders can be at descending, considering the fact that they do it for a living. It's all relative, of course, and they'd still drop an amateur no problem, but the skill gap between the best and the worst descenders is incredible. I feel bad singling out anyone in particular because there are a few who could really up their game, but the Portuguese rider Tiago Machado or the Austrian Riccardo Zoidl were two who made bad impressions on me during races. If you're behind someone like that, you're going to be dropped. Zoidl is a talented climber and he's only thirty one, but I think the fact that he was so slow downhill played a part in him losing his spot with Trek-Segafredo and having to go back to an Austrian Continental team. Given his talents elsewhere, Andy Schleck was a surprisingly poor descender. Not all the time, but if he'd had a crash recently or if the conditions were bad, he'd constantly be tapping his brakes and second-guessing himself.

Some of the WorldTour teams will work with downhill coaches, and mountain biking has definitely helped me improve, so it is something that every rider can work on even as they get older. It helps if you've done lots of it from an early age, but with a little work on things like racing lines and keeping focused, you can make big improvements quickly. A lot of the crashes I've had in the past were just that – losing my concentration at the worst possible moment. When I worked with a coach on that, he stressed the importance of training myself to stay attentive the whole way down, and to have confidence in the lines I take. If you worry too much and start to make little adjustments as you're cornering, you're going to do more harm than good most of the time. And if you're too heavy on the brakes, it's going to have a seriously detrimental effect on your times. A skilful rider might not actually make up that much time on a descent in the grand scheme of things, but the big advantage he'll have is that he'll be fresh at the bottom because the whole way down he's just coasting comfortably, pedalling regularly, braking as little as possible, maintaining momentum. A poor descender will slam on his brakes into every bend, probably make an adjustment or two in the middle of the turn, and then have to stand up out of the saddle and sprint to regain his speed. Riding like that is going to wear you out.

Bernie Eisel's head injuries were scary, because it was six weeks after he'd crashed before they knew how serious it was. He suffered a subdural haematoma, bleeding on the brain, when he went down during the Tirreno Adriatico in March 2018. But he was also lucky to catch it, because originally they thought that he'd escaped with just a fractured wrist. Then he felt bad, so he went for a scan. I think there is always going to be some risk involved in a sport like cycling, and there will always be close calls like that one, but on the whole I don't think it's anything to worry about too much, especially when you compare it to boxing or American football. I wouldn't like to have been racing back in the old days when they didn't have to wear helmets though. The idea of being allowed to take them off for the final climb on mountaintop finishes is nice because the photos would look better and it would be a little more comfortable, but I can't see it happening.

In terms of what happens directly after a crash, there's a worrying lack of protocol, in my opinion. If there's a doctor there, he can check you out, but most of the time we just pick up our bikes and get moving again, especially if it's late in a stage and the tempo is high. Even in a relatively safe sport like football, there are protocols for concussion and head injuries and it's worthwhile because not only are they taking care of the player's current, short-term injuries, but it also makes it less likely that he'll develop issues in later life. And you can see how badly even a small knock can affect someone's performance. I remember being shocked at how bad Loris Karius was in goal for Liverpool during the 2018 Champions League final, he looked drunk, or like someone who had never kicked a ball in his life. Sergio Ramos, the Real Madrid defender, had hit him in the head but the referee didn't do anything about it. And then it came out a couple of days after the game that he had felt unwell while on holiday in the United States, so he went for a scan. He'd suffered a concussion and shouldn't even have been on the pitch. I'd like to see more care being taken in cycling, but I have to admit, I'm not sure how you do it. You can't ban crashing. It's part of the job. A shitty part, but it's still an inevitable occupational hazard when you race bikes for a living.

I think some riders would like to see more defined controls on the motorbikes within races, too. Personally, I think they're all there to do a job, either as part of the media or the race organisation, and they're professionals with a lot of experience. I've noticed in recent years that they seem to be blamed for a lot, which I think is unfair. It definitely varies from race to race, but on the whole I don't think they're as big a problem as people make them out to be. At a small race, maybe there's an issue with inexperience, but the TV motorbike pilots in France and Italy have been doing it a long time. I remember there being some issues at the 2018 Vuelta when some breakaways were effectively closed down by riders drafting motorbikes, but that's just poor organisation, so I don't pay much attention to the people who say that they should be banned from the races or have their numbers reduced. There are a lot of bikes that need to be there as part of the race jury, or to ride ahead of the race alongside the police bikes to make sure the route is ready, and then there are the TV cameras and the photographers, who we need to promote the sport. So there isn't really an alternative. Once the race organisers control them properly, I think they're fine. They're just part of the circus.

It's about defining an acceptable level of risk. If you're racing a bike, you have to accept the risk that you might crash at high-speed. That's inescapable. But do we have to accept that after that crash, a rider should be expected to decline proper medical examination in favour of continuing? A big issue is the fact that we, the riders, feel like we always have to get back on the bike. I think it was the same in rugby before they changed their rules. Now if you watch a game, you'll see players being examined carefully before being allowed back on the pitch, and if needs be, you'll see a big-name player sitting out a match for the sake of his own safety. I'm sure that's frustrating, because when you compete for a living you never want to be left out, but it's a sensible move.

The prevailing mentality is that if you stop for anything less than a broken leg, or the fact that you're unconscious in the back of an ambulance, you're soft. That's ridiculous. I still shiver when I think of seeing Toms Skujins' crash at the 2017 Tour of California. The Cannondale-Drapac rider hit the ground hard while in a breakaway, and then stumbled around trying to get back on his bike. When he fell over, a neutral support mechanic inspected the bike and was ready to give it back to him, until Skujins stumbled to the other side of the road, struggling to pick up his glasses before walking right out into the oncoming chase group. When he eventually made it back to the mechanic, he was given his bike and sent on his merry way, almost crashing right into a kerb shortly after. Eventually, his team car caught up to him and convinced him to retire, and later that day he was diagnosed with a concussion along with a broken collarbone. And during the 2018 Tour de France, Philippe Gilbert had a horrible crash, flew over a wall into a ditch, and then got up and rode to the finish line 60 kilometres away – with a fractured knee cap. He got the day's combativity prize and a lot of praise from fans and the media for being hard, but for what? There's a perverse voyeurism to cycling sometimes, and I think it needs to end. He was lucky that it was just his knee, because with the current attitude in cycling, if he'd hit his head but insisted on getting back on his bike, he would have been allowed to. I know how that feels, I've been in that situation, and particularly if there was a win on the cards, you'd need to drag me away to stop me from racing. One solution would be more medical staff, but I don't see where we could fit them in. Team cars are crammed already with equipment, food, and bottles. There's hardly enough space for the mechanic and his tools. And the last thing the peloton needs is more vehicles getting in the way. But if the rules were clearer, and we perhaps tried something simple like impact indicators on helmets to give an idea of how hard the fall had been, riders would learn to accept a new restriction that would ultimately be in their best interest.

Until something like that happens, some of the responsibility in terms of safety also has to go to the riders. When push comes to shove, it's us who set the pace of the race. I get a kick out of it sometimes when we absolutely hammer one another on a big climb at the Giro or the Tour. I think to myself, 'This could have been so civilised, but here we are, going hell for leather', and it makes me smile. It's the old way of racing. All it takes is one guy to light the match and the whole thing explodes, regardless of what the plan had been beforehand.

I'm probably a bit old-school in my thinking about the dangers, saying that it's just part of the job and we should get on with it, but I've also seen a big change in the style of racing over the course of my career. The descents were always dangerous, it's not like the race organisers have magically conjured up these new downhill sections out of thin air. The potential for disaster was always there, but when I was young, it used to be a lot more controlled. I can remember Liquigas, in particular, absolutely hammering everyone on the climb, only to ease off the gas for a minute or two after the summit so that everyone could regroup for the descent. Partly that was because Ivan Basso wasn't the best descender and he didn't want to take too many risks, knowing that he could beat almost anyone on the uphill, but it was also a respect thing. There was a mutual respect between all the teams and the riders. Now, that's gone out the window. Sky will attack on the descents, UAE will attack, it never lets up. It creates so much stress in the bunch because on those narrow roads, we're stuck for space and at high speeds, there's really only a small sliver of tarmac that's the 'right' place to be. We're all fighting for position, overtaking in dangerous sections, taking risks that don't really need to be taken. I understand that it's become a good tactic for some of the general classification riders to attack on the descent, like Vincenzo Nibali or Chris Froome, and it's an admirable and very technical skill to have, but when every single rider in the race is trying to do the same it puts us in too much danger. It's thrilling to watch when two riders who are good at it go man to man, but there are others who totally suck at it and yet they'll follow them anyway. To me, that's like Andre Greipel trying to chase Julian Alaphilippe up a climb.

Guys like David de la Cruz, Thibaut Pinot, Sébastien Reichenbach, all talented riders at big teams, but if you're behind them at the top of a climb you're going to get gapped pretty quickly unless you pass them because they can't descend at all. The first word that would come to mind if I found myself on their wheel on a descent would be 'fuck', because I'd know straight away that it's a bad position to be in. If you stick with a rider like that, you'll be pulling like crazy for five or six kilometres at the bottom just to re-join the bunch. In my first few years as a pro, the bad descenders didn't get gapped like that, because the whole peloton used to descend at a reasonable speed. Sometimes I wonder if it's because of a false sense of security, knowing that the modern helmets are so much better than they used to be, but mostly I just put it down to the fact that the top guys are all so close these days when it comes to climbing ability that they have to make a difference elsewhere.

Of course, there are some things that you just can't plan for. Look at what happened to poor Michael Goolaerts in the 2018 Paris–Roubaix. He crashed suddenly in the second sector of pavé, near to Briastre. The race doctors treated him because he was unconscious, and then he was airlifted to a hospital in Lille, where he died that night. The autopsy showed that he suffered a cardiac arrest before he crashed, rather than because of it. He was only twenty-three. He was from just over the border in Belgium so riding his first Paris–Roubaix must have been a dream for him.

I can't begin to imagine what that night must have been like for his team. They'd carried on racing, because that's what you do. At that moment, you're not thinking the worst. You're not thinking straight at all. It's full race mode, for the riders and the team directors, so you're thinking about position in the group, flat tyres, breaks. Looking back on that after hearing he'd died, I know that must have been devastating for his team.

To be honest, it was devastating for us all. It's not like the guys who were smiling as they crossed the line, or who were up on the podium celebrating, could have known anything, but when you hear that news and you think about the way you enjoyed yourself, it's human nature to feel regretful and sad about it.

The Verandas Willems–Crelan riders were back racing that week at the Brabantse Pijl Flanders Classic in his honour. That must have been incredibly difficult, but there was nothing they could do. If a colleague from your office passes away, it's not like the business closes its doors until everyone recovers from the loss. It seems more callous in the context of sport because it's high-profile, but at the end of the day, the team has commitments and salaries to pay, and sending everyone home for a month isn't going to help those riders or the staff in the long run.

It was disgusting to see some people suggest a link to doping in the press and on social media. There was no evidence of anything other than heart failure, and yet some people couldn't help themselves. They had to bring up doping. Cardiac arrest is tragically common in elite-level sports, because the heart undergoes structural changes as a result of high-performance training. It happened to the Italian footballer Davide Astori in 2018, and over the years I can remember several similar cases both in cycling and in sports in general.

I hope that more research is done into that condition, and that the governing bodies and teams can figure out a way to accurately test athletes for symptoms, but ultimately, it's not something that scares me. Tragedies like that happen in normal life too, and you can't walk around being scared of everything all the time. Crashes are the only thing I worry about. When Wouter Weylandt crashed and died at the 2011 Giro d'Italia, that affected us deeply. He was descending at around 80km/h and looked back, and in a split second he hit the leading edge of a guardrail and it was over. The doctors said he died instantly from the impact, his heart stopped and he had severe head injuries. That's a side of cycling you just can't get away from. Modern helmets are really good, but they can't work miracles. There's a reason that motorcycle helmets weigh ten times more than a bicycle helmet, and those guys wear leather with armour plates as well.

The heart issue is really sad because they are young guys in the prime of life. We're tested a lot and I trust that our doctors are doing the best that can be done, so there's no point worrying about it. These things can happen no matter what you do for a job. I've heard people saying that the stresses we put our bodies under end up causing damage, but I don't believe that. And anyway, how can it be worse than sitting at a desk all day? Cycling can be dangerous, but not because of heart attacks. I'm not going to tell my kid not to ride a bike because it might cause heart problems. Some of my friends don't like road biking because they're afraid of the cars, so they stick to mountain biking and off-road trails, but I couldn't live my life like that. I've been hit by cars before, and it sucks, but bad things can happen on a mountain bike as well. Just look at Martyn Ashton, he was a legend in the mountain biking scene but a crash in 2013 dislocated his T9 and T10 vertebrae, and now he's a paraplegic. If that can happen to one of the best in the world, it can happen to anyone. Is it a reason not to ride? I don't think so. I read that around 6,000 pedestrians are killed every year on American roads, but it's not like you're going to stop walking around.

The medical support at the races is good, for the most part. I've had one or two bad experiences, but that also depends on what part of the world you're racing in. I remember being in one ambulance and I knew that I'd broken bones because I was in so much pain. There was damage done to my ribcage too, but they discharged me right after the examination and told me it was safe to fly home. I took a load of painkillers and had a couple of glasses of wine, and when I woke up the next morning I felt like death. The team sent me to get checked out by my own doctor, and it turned out that on top of a broken hand and some fractured ribs, I had a partially collapsed lung. You're not even supposed to fly with that. But that's not the race organiser's fault – that was a big hospital. I'm just glad I don't live nearby with that place as my local. When I heard my doctor's diagnosis, I was actually happy in a weird way, because when they'd told me that I was fine the day before I felt like a wimp because I was in so much pain. All I could think was, 'I knew I was fucked up!'

MECHANICAL WONDERS

Let's not use the term 'mechanical doping'. It's dumb. You're not doping by adding an engine to your bicycle, you're turning it into a motorbike. It's the kind of cheating that is so deplorable that calling it 'doping' is, in some perverse way, actually offensive to the old-fashioned frauds who took drugs to gain an advantage. I'm joking, obviously. I don't want to defend the dopers. But they still actually did the work, albeit with pharmaceutical help. If there's someone in the peloton today that can't even be bothered to pedal on his own, that's another level of deceit.

The story about Femke Van den Driessche shocked the pro riders I know as much as it did the general public. In case you missed it, she was the Belgian rider who was found with a motor in her bike at the women's under-23 race of the Cyclocross World Championships in January 2016. The UCI found the motor and a battery concealed in the seat tube, thanks to magnetic resonance testing. For the record, the governing body call this 'technological fraud', which, I think, is a much better name. A little Bluetooth switch was hidden away under her bar tape. It's insane to think that a nineteen-year-old kid could be that corrupt already, especially as she had already won U-23 Belgian and European cyclocross championships. How long had she been cheating? The family claimed that the bike belonged to a friend of theirs and that, because Van den Driessche had sold it to him the year before, it was identical to her one. They claimed that it was simply a case of mistaken identity, and that a mechanic had cleaned

it and put it with Van den Driessche's other bikes by accident. Then it came out that at the same time as this case
was going on her brother was serving a ban for doping, while
also facing criminal charges along with his father for stealing
expensive parakeets from a shop somewhere in Flanders. It
was such an odd story. I remember reading an April Fool's
Day article a couple of months later that reported on her
leveraging the scandal to promote a return to cycling competition at a mountain-bike race for e-bikes, and thinking,
'I could almost believe that.'

Rumours about this kind of thing have been around far
longer than Van den Driessche. There was Fabian Cancellara's
attack on Tom Boonen on the Kapelmuur to win the 2010
Ronde van Vlaanderen, and a strange video of Ryder Hesjedal's
bike at the 2014 Vuelta a España, which seemed to show it
moving around of its own accord after the Canadian crashed
while cornering. In Italy, a special prosecutor actually investigated claims about motors in bikes at professional races
dating as far back as 2004, when Van den Driessche would
have been eight.

That investigation came about because Davide Cassani, a
retired pro rider turned television presenter, did a feature about
a concealed motor that the producer claimed had been used
in races. These days, Cassani is probably best known as the
manager of the Italian national cycling team but he had a solid
career as a domestique during the glory days of the Carerra
team, supporting the likes of Roberto Visentini and Stephen
Roche, before going on to win a couple of stages at the Giro
d'Italia during the early 1990s. Unwittingly, he was also the
man responsible for Michael Rasmussen's doping downfall back
in 2007, when he made a casual remark about seeing the
Danish rider training hard in the Italian Dolomites – when
Rasmussen had claimed to be in Mexico. I mention all of this

just to say that Cassani is a respected figure in cycling with a lot of connections and experience both as a racer and as a journalist, so I'm sure there was a good reason for him to take the motor story seriously, but I have a hard time believing it.

Thinking that maybe I was being naïve, I've been talking to as many other pros about it as possible, and the consensus seems to be that it isn't an issue. Even guys that rode with Cancellara and weren't big fans don't believe it. Cancellara might not be everyone's cup of tea, but the guy is a legend: four time-trial world championships, plenty of stage wins at the Tour de France and Vuelta a España, a win at Milano–Sanremo, and three titles each at Paris–Roubaix and the Ronde van Vlaanderen in a generation that included Tom Boonen. He had sixteen podiums at the Monuments in the decade between 2006 and 2016. It's an incredible feat, and that's without mentioning his victories at other prestigious one-day races like the Strade Bianche and E3 Harelbeke.

I was surprised to see Phil Gaimon giving it so much attention in his book, *Draft Animals*. I like Gaimon's writing, most of the time, anyway. But on this issue I think he was really unfair. He starts off by dragging up old rumours about Cancellara being a client of the Spanish doping doctor Eufemiano Fuentes who was at the centre of the Operation Puerto case back in 2006. When police raided property belonging to Fuentes, they found large stashes of doping paraphernalia, and a number of bags filled with blood, each with its own codename. The scandal engulfed a lot of big names in the peloton and speculation was rife that one of the bags – 'No. 24 Clasicómano Luigi' – belonged to Cancellara, but no evidence of his involvement was ever found, and in 2016, Thomas Dekker admitted that he'd been 'Clasicómano Luigi' all along. The Dutch rider confirmed that fact almost a year before Gaimon's book was released, and Phil was aware of it because he discussed it on Twitter and mentioned it in the book's afterword, but for some reason the American decided to stick the old bit of gossip in there anyway, before adding that he believed Cancellara's bike had been rigged with a motor (a claim Cancellara has fervently denied), allowing the Swiss to 'ride away from a "who's who" of dopers.' That's a big claim to put into print.

The fact that someone was caught using a motor at the Cyclocross World Championships made me re-evaluate my opinion of technological fraud. If it's been caught at a big race, you'd have to assume it's not the first time someone's done it. At the same time though, I have never come across anything that could be seriously considered by a big team or rider in professional road racing. For one thing, the motors I've seen are loud enough to be heard, and when you're surrounded by almost 200 riders and dozens of TV cameras – including some small ones now being mounted on bikes for in-race footage – the risk of being seen by someone pressing the button seems too dicey for even the most desperate to try. Some people might counter that and say that guys were willing to take huge gambles with their health to dope, and that's true, but until recently they could be fairly certain that they wouldn't get caught doing it unless they showed up at the start line with a syringe in their arse. All it would take is one curious glance in the bunch, or an observant cameraman, and your entire career would be ruined.

There's also the logistics of it. If you want to go get some drugs, you can make that decision solo. If you're putting a motor in your bike, at the very least one of the mechanics would need to know, and given the way teams work, more than likely all of them would need to be in on it. It makes no sense for them. They're in this for the long haul, they want to hold on to their job as long as they can, and it's different for them, they're not like riders, for whom one win can make all the difference. Once they work hard, their job is safe, or at least, as safe as anyone's job can be in professional cycling. And even with a mechanic's assistance, I don't see how they could guarantee secrecy, because privacy is in very short supply at bike races and it's very hard to do anything totally out of view. In my opinion, you'd need the whole team on board, from the other riders to the soigneurs and directors, to even consider it, and you'd better hope you never get caught because I think any big pro caught adding a motor to his frame will find himself slapped with a lawsuit by the bike company quicker than any little engine can carry him.

As an analogy, Lance Armstrong's doping hurt Trek, his bike sponsor, as much as it hurt everyone else around him, but it didn't incriminate them. Their bikes were still awesome, they just happened to be used by a cheater. If he'd been caught using a motor to win those Tours, the implications for a bike company would be far more serious, and the subsequent response far more aggressive. I don't know how effective the UCI's magnetic testing machines are, or how eagerly they're looking, but even now, with all of the controls like the biological passport and the whereabouts checks, I still think it would be less dangerous to just dope if you're intent on cheating.

There was a CBS News documentary a while back, interviewing a Hungarian engineer by the name of Istvan Varjas, who insisted that motors had actually been used in pro racing since the 1990s, and that he'd sold his unique design to a mystery buyer for $2 million. A lot of the reports seem to stem from him. He also claimed that, rather than a motor at the cranks, riders were now using a sophisticated system based on magnets in the rear wheel. The science sounds convincing, until you think that anyone – a teammate, someone from the UCI, a journalist – can randomly pick up a bike at a race and if there's an extra kilo of magnets in the super-light carbon-fibre rear wheel, they're going to feel it right away because the bike would be totally off-balance, and around 15 per cent heavier than you'd expect it to be.

I've never seen anything advanced enough to be undetectable in that kind of situation. And knowing how desperate the bike industry is to sell you shit that you do not need, my honest feeling is that if someone was able to make one, you'd be able to buy one. That's how cycling works. If there's a market for €1,000 carbon-fibre shoes and gold-plated titanium wheel hubs, then there's a market for motors. It's crazy just to think about though. I can get my head around someone doping, but using a motor is another thing. That said, the television reports look believable and newspapers like the *Gazzetta dello Sport* and the *Corriere della Sera* in Italy, or *L'Équipe* and *Le Monde* in France, are respectable publications. I don't think these venerable old institutions are going to start making things up about bike racing just to attract a few clicks online.

Everyone I've ever talked to about it has said that it's worse than doping. You have to wonder how much honour really exists among thieves, and if someone is willing to dope, why wouldn't they be willing to use a motor, but the reaction I always get is that it's the next level of cheating, you're taking it away from being a physical competition. I think no matter how much someone doped, they could always convince themselves that it was really them winning the races. But it would take a superhuman talent for cognitive dissonance to look yourself in the mirror and say you won legitimately with an electric engine pushing the cranks. And yet still, when I see riders changing bikes in the middle of a race, I can't help but wonder.

Cancellara's reaction to Gaimon's book seemed reasonable enough to me. The whole situation came across as childish at first, with the two of them sniping at one another on Twitter, but I'd have come back at him in a less friendly way if he said the same thing about me. Eventually, they became friendly and raced one another at a publicity event in Switzerland. Gaimon was raising money for his charity and Cancellara was promoting his own granfondo, and it looked like it was very amiable. The American won, but in fairness to the Swiss, it was on a seven-kilometre climb. Maybe they should have round two on the cobbles in Belgium.

SEXISM

I don't want to keep going back to *Draft Animals*, but I can't let this point go unmentioned. There's a lot of pontificating going on in that book when it comes to morality, and it seems like Phil Gaimon has spent a lot of time sharing his sanctimonious opinions on cycling, but just a paragraph after accusing Cancellara of being a cheat, Phil casually jokes about David Zabriskie and Lachlan Morton exchanging tips on how to look up women's skirts. It's one of several examples of overtly sexist 'banter' in the book that just doesn't sit right. If it came from someone like Mario Cipollini, I'd expect it, but it's hard to swallow all of the sanctimony from someone who thinks it's funny to leer at women because that, to me, is a more relevant threat to the image of cycling than any scheme to hide little motors.

Thankfully, I don't believe that kind of mentality is so prevalent any more, at least not with the riders I know. There's been a total shift since I became a pro. All of the guys on my team now are clever, thoughtful people. Most of us have studied a bit and our backgrounds are much more diverse. Back in the early 2000s you'd never see so many people reading books at a training camp. Cycling in Europe has always been a working-class sport, but there are more opportunities for young people now to get a good education no matter where they're from, and I think that education is given more value by young athletes and the people around them than it used to be. In a certain way, it was almost cool to be ignorant back in the day, but none of these young guys want to be seen as a meathead.

My old teammates used to come to camp with a bag full of pornography. We'd be at the dinner table and guys would be comparing and trading their collections of dirty magazines. It's a lot more sophisticated than that now, guys will talk about books and films but if someone brought up porn I think some of them would die from shock. When I turned pro, the old guard in the team actually had a couple of groupies who'd follow them around most of the European races, and whenever they were bored, the girls would be invited over to the hotel for a night. I also remember hearing horror stories about a woman that they called 'The Beast of Diksmuide', after the Flemish town where she lived. Apparently, she had a big thing for soigneurs, so at races like Gent–Wevelgem, they couldn't wait to get to the feeding zone because she'd be there waiting for them an hour before the peloton arrived.

Stories like that used to be so common. And there were a lot of guys who loved that image. I don't know how many women Cipollini claims to have slept with, but when I was younger I heard impressive things about an old French pro, who allegedly had a female admirer or two in every town we visited during the Tour de France. Team directors used to leave their wives at home and bring their girlfriends – and no one would bat an eyelid. They'd stay at the hotel with us, eat dinner with us, and everyone would know what was going on. I can think of one of the big Classics teams where it's still going on. In the old days, it wasn't unusual for the DS or the manager to use some of the drugs that the riders were taking. Picture that, your boss, this older guy who you're supposed to respect, and he's flying around like a ball of energy, and super-horny, because he was using the testosterone patches. When I was young, guys would boast about their exploits, but the mentality has changed and so has the everyday reality. We don't party hard any more, we're more boring, which given cycling's delinquent past, maybe isn't such a bad thing. There wasn't any particular moment that you could pinpoint and say, 'That's when cycling changed', it's just been something that's evolved in recent years and I'm happy to say that the bunch is a more enlightened place now. There's certainly no more Beast of Diksmuide, at least that I know of.

One year at the Vuelta a Burgos, a stage race in northern Spain, one of the team hotels was right beside a brothel, and the next morning at breakfast all the talk was about the girls and what some of the guys had gotten up to. That would never happen now – you'd be called a dickhead straight away. The attitude was different. When I came into the sport, it was all just part of an image. They saw themselves as bandits on the road, they took drugs and fucked hookers and they were proud of it.

There's a lot of things that I'd like to see change in cycling, but it's hard for me to take the journalists seriously when they start talking about sexism these days. Where were they back in the early 2000s? There were definitely a few riders you could have named and shamed back then. But I still hear some people talking about Peter Sagan at the 2013 Tour of Flanders when he pinched a podium girl's backside. It was immature and insensitive, but in fairness to Peter, it was not the dumbest thing any twenty-three-year-old has ever done. Personally, I think the podium girl thing is a relic of the past, but that has nothing to do with the riders or the teams. The people who are asking for those girls and hiring them are civilians who own successful business and who sponsor the events, so I don't like when people say that it's a problem with cycling. Should those paymasters tell the race organisers that they want kids, local dignitaries, or a trained animal to present the prizes, they'd do it as long as the money was good. So if it's a brand of prosecco or a beer company who are paying these girls to stand around in revealing clothing, then I think it's more accurate to say that it's a problem with the drinks industry. At the same time, it's also fair to say that no one is forcing those women to do that, so perhaps before the rest of us decide what's best for them, they should be consulted. Either way, it's not something that riders care about.

Women's racing is a different matter. The sport has come on in leaps and bounds since I turned pro and I hope that it continues to grow. I'm not an expert, but the women's teams are getting bigger and as race organisers start to create more space for them, we get to see more of one another at events like Strade Bianche in Tuscany and the big Belgian Classics. It's brilliant to race for the same crowds and when I get a chance to watch their races on TV I enjoy them because they have their own style. It's less tactical most of the time, but with plenty of energy and excitement. I'm not proud to admit it, but I was sceptical when I was younger. It wasn't based on anything, just a youthful cluelessness and the rub of uneducated attitudes that prevailed in the bunch back then. I want to coach, for example, and would love to work with younger athletes, but a few years ago I would have turned my nose up at girls because I had this silly idea that they'd always be moaning and not willing to work hard. Part of that could also have been because I'd never seen them competing at a high level, it was only local events and they weren't that serious. But now when you see the WorldTour teams, they're total badasses. I can't think of a better word for them. They train so hard, act so professional, and go to every race wanting to win. I could make a sizeable list of guys from the bunch who could learn a thing or two from that attitude.

No doubt there are challenges. I don't think the race organisers or the teams should be forced to do anything they don't want to. This is professional sport, and professional sport has its own perversely egalitarian outlook that I don't think you can control. We get paid what the market deems we're worth, and the public watches what it deems worth watching. Forcing teams to have a women's squad might sound good on paper, but it won't help anyone if that team then has to fold after a year or two because of budget problems.

It's true that the sport could do a lot more to get people at home watching women's racing, but talk to a manager at the Pro Continental men's team and he'll tell you that they have the same problem. There's so much variety on television these days that most sports fans only want to watch the very biggest events, with the fastest riders. That's not a gender thing, that's just because they're spoiled for choice, and if a race doesn't have Chris Froome and Vincenzo Nibali battling it out for the GC, they can just switch channels and watch football, Moto GP, or Formula One. If we want to build a market for women's cycling then I think we need to widen the net, because a large section of cycling's current support base is not going to suddenly start watching women's racing when they can't be bothered to watch most of the races on the men's calendar. Viewer numbers and race attendances are healthy at the marquee events like the Classics and the Grand Tours, but since I've turned pro we've lost loads of great races across Europe that were steeped in history and charm, but that just couldn't make ends meet.

Mitchelton–Scott and Team Sunweb have women's teams and that's encouraging, but I don't think anyone should fool themselves into thinking that those teams came into being for purely altruistic reasons. They've figured out a way to make that work financially and they should be applauded for that, because on the amateur side, the female share of the market is the sport's big growth area and it's smart of them to get in there. It's important to remember, however, that these aren't charitable organisations or teams that are being funded with taxpayers' money, so whatever setup they choose to support is totally up to them. I remember Emma Pooley complaining about the fact that no one had tried to set up something like Team Sky for women, and I agree with her that at that time more could have been done in the UK to create a women's team because they had some incredible results at the Olympics, but at the end of the day, what Rupert Murdoch chooses to do with his millions is his own business. Rather than focus on the negative, I'd rather point to the success of Wiggle High5, a British team that has become a major force on the women's WorldTour. It's also worth pointing out that when Rabobank pulled its money from the Netherlands' major men's team in 2012 following a litany of doping scandals, they carried on with the women's team for another four years because they obviously saw value – and values – there that deserved their investment.

It also probably didn't hurt that Marianne Vos was the most dominant cyclist in the world at the time, male or female. With a rider like that, seven times World Cyclocross Champion and three times World Road Race Champion, capable of winning big Classics and stage races, any team is good value for a sponsor but it's comical how little it costs to run a women's cycling outfit. You could run the biggest women's team in the world for a decade on what even the most frugal men's WorldTour team spends in a season. If I were in that position as a sponsor, right now, I think I'd rather go with the women because it's so cheap and there's so much potential.

Growing the races should be an organic process as well, in my opinion, because when you see big organisers like RCS in Italy cancelling an event like Roma Maxima, a race that has an eighty-year history and a lot of prestige, it's clear that it isn't possible any more to hold a race if it's going to lose money. Where it's been successful – Flanders, Flèche Wallonne, Amstel

Gold Race, the Strade Bianche – they have gained a following because the races captivate the audience's imagination, and they've proven to the organisers that there's added value. The point is that, the development of cycling shouldn't be a battle of the sexes, or an argument that can be reduced down to haves and have nots. It should be about improving the sport as a whole and making it a more interesting product for sponsors and fans alike. If we can achieve that, the tide will raise all boats.

BEING A FAN

Cycling appeals for a lot of reasons. There's the speed of it, the tactics, the unpredictability inherent in a group of almost 200 athletes, all desperate to win, all willing to take incredible risks. The weather can turn a race on its head without warning, and a crash can derail even the most meticulously laid plans. The favourite's form means nothing if he hits the deck at 100 kilometres per hour. Then there's the human scale of it: we're not in a stadium or something you observe from a distance or from behind glass. The fans can get right up close as we climb those famous mountains and see the expressions on our faces as we wring every gram of power out of our bodies and struggle against gravity and waves of exhaustion. And when the race is over, they're free to go down to the bottom and try it for themselves, without waiting in a queue or having to go anywhere to buy a ticket. The road is there, and all are welcome to it.

Sometimes, those fans can get too close. It's a complaint that you hear often from riders during the biggest races, but it's not because we hate the fans or expect to compete inside a bubble. It's just that when you're on the bleeding edge of what's physically possible and a whole season, maybe a career, is hanging in the balance, you don't want it messed up by some dickhead in a costume who's had too much to drink and is only thinking of getting on television.

At a race like the Tour de France or the Giro d'Italia, the fans are everywhere, from morning until night. They'll be in the hotel lobby, outside the bus before the start, crowding the sign-on area, lining the roads, and then they'll swarm the finish the second the supervising police let their guard down. It's non-stop. And if you're having a bad day, you'll moan about it, but you don't really mean it. It's a bit like seeing a friend or a neighbour waving and smiling from across the street when you just want to mind your own business. It's not them, it's you.

Mountaintop finishes can be a problem, because there can be thousands of fans up there with little or nothing to separate us all. After the line, the riders have to navigate their way through throngs of people, hoping that no one will bump into you or start pulling at your jersey. People don't realise it but sometimes we'll be in pain, maybe from a crash a few days previous, and they'll be patting us on the back to congratulate us, but at the same time torturing some poor bastard who has a bruised rib or whose sides are covered in road rash. You might be trying to get to the bus quickly because it's freezing or lashing down rain, and there'll be hundreds of people in the way, enjoying the spectacle of it all and trying to spot their favourite riders, not noticing that it's cold or wet because they're not drenched in a skin-tight outfit that weighs 300 grams. You have to stop yourself from screaming sometimes.

Coming down off a mountain, when the space at the top is too tight for all the teams to park the buses, is even worse. You want to go fast, but there'll be people walking in every direction, cyclists riding up, someone's kid in the middle of the road. I know a few guys who carry whistles, and we'll just blow them as hard as we can while we shoot down. It works pretty well. I remember passing a couple of guys from Team Sky at the Tour a few years ago and they were blocked by a group of fans who all moved when they heard the whistle. I pointed to it in my mouth and joked, 'Hey guys, marginal gains!' I don't know if they found it funny or not. Imagine the final of the Champions League or the World Cup, and at the end of the match, all the players had to walk for ten or fifteen minutes outside the stadium to get to their changing rooms. It's inconceivable, but that's the reality in cycling. Obviously, the locations make it next to impossible to accommodate everyone, and none of that chaos is the fan's fault because they're just having fun and without them none of us would have jobs, but I do wonder why the race organisers don't do more to improve the situation. I don't see the top brass from ASO or RCS having to hang about in the rain or walk a couple of kilometres to get to their cars.

All of that is just a minor headache in the heat of the moment, when we're tired and hungry and possibly covered in road rash. I love the fans. I'm a fan. I've done stages at the Vuelta a España, racing up a huge mountain, and no one was there. It differs region by region, and geography plays a huge part because some parts of that race are very isolated, but a lot of the time, the Spanish fans just don't turn out like the French and Italians. That's a weird sensation, like it somehow matters less. You're not used to seeing that kind of road without all the colour and the noise that the fans bring – we feed off that energy. At the finish, or when we're doing a crit in some little town where it seems like every single one of the inhabitants has come out to see the race, I feel like apologising to everyone because I can't stop to do autographs. You'd be there all day, and we're under strict instructions to get showered and changed as quickly as possible so we don't get sick, and to begin our recovery. I know it seems arrogant when I just roll by, but trust me, most of the guys in the bunch would love to hang around because it feels good when everyone is cheering for you like that.

Occasionally, you'll meet a guy who has no time for the fans, like he's special. But that's not the norm. That's why so many fans love Peter Sagan, for example, because that guy engages with the public. Even when he's not popping wheelies, he takes the time to wave and smile. It takes a second but means a lot. It's harder when you're in a part of the world that really loves bike racing, the heartlands in Belgium or the Netherlands or northern Italy. Even a small rider is a celebrity there and everyone wants to talk to you or take a picture. The big stars will come home from training and find someone outside their house hoping to catch a glimpse of him. That's difficult to manage and a lot of guys just zone out, even with their friends. They're there, but they're not there. When that happens, I won't even bother with small talk, I'll just catch up with them in the hotel later for a proper chat. Training somewhere like the US, or doing the Tour of California, is great for that. The hardcore roadies will know you, but no one else because cycling isn't so massive there. You can go out for lunch or a beer with some friends and you're just like anyone else. Maybe they're looking at me wondering why I'm so skinny, but they've no idea that in a couple of months' time I'll be racing the Tour de France, this monster of an event that gets something like 1.5 billion viewers each year.

Fans change by region, too. It might sound funny, but it's the truth. Italian fans will be really knowledgeable and passionate. That's a stereotype but if you've ever seen a football game or a bike race there, you know what I mean. They're running alongside the road screaming like they've lost their minds. They can be partisan, they come to see their guys, but if you're a good rider they'll respect you no matter where you're from. The average people in little restaurants or in hotels will be really proud to have you there, especially if your team is leading the Giro d'Italia. Most of them are family-run establishments, I guess, so they take a lot of pride in having someone special in their place. The only annoying thing about racing in Italy is the kids howling at you, *'Borraccia! Borraccia!'* because they want the water bottles. Sometimes the adults are like that too! At the 2017 Giro, the Czech rider Michal Schlegel got his bottle stolen by a fan from the cage on his bike … while he was racing up Mount Etna. It makes me laugh because it's so insane, the kind of thing that could only happen in cycling. In northern Europe, the Belgians will know everything about you, but don't want to talk much, they might just say, 'Hey, good luck tomorrow.' The Dutch usually try to be funny with you, making jokes you've heard a hundred times before and expecting a laugh. You'll try to grab a coffee somewhere the day before a race and no matter where you go, there'll be some smartarse asking you why you're not out training. And the French, well, it probably won't surprise you when I say that most of them don't give a shit. Or, at least, they pretend not to.

At the height of your career, when you're winning, it can be stressful. When you're a neo-pro or a domestique, you can ride around and no one will bother you. If you want to wash your bike, you can do it in the front garden, no problem. The neighbours might say hello but that will be it. Once you make a name for yourself though, it all changes. Fans will start to track you down, and even that neighbour who used to say a polite hello and then go about his business is now coming over to talk about racing and what you're doing. It's part of the gig, of course, but it's tiring to be constantly in the public eye. Big riders can seem aloof and unfriendly, but they're forced into that position. You expect it at the races, but not at home when you're just trying to take the kids to the park. You can't do the coffee stop any more on a ride with friends, you just start drinking it at home instead. Sometimes it works to your advantage, when you get a table in a full cafe or the waiter notices you at a restaurant, but mostly it's just exhausting.

The first time you experience it, though, it's all amazing. My first Grand Tour I was part of the winning team, and I didn't want to leave because I loved being the centre of attention.

I was able to signal to someone in the hotel and they'd bring me coffee right away, they wanted to do everything for us, and then I had to go home where I couldn't just click my fingers and expect a cappuccino. Nobody in my house is asking me for an autograph.

It's an addiction. I can feel it now, tugging at me, because I know that before too long I won't be able to get a fix of it any more. During the Tour, I could really notice it. I needed it. My wife even saw it in me, the craving for adrenalin and action. The tactical part of racing still consumes me, and I love the social aspect of it, spending twenty-four hours a day with this close-knit group of guys who'd do anything for one another. I hope that when I call it a day, I'll get another kind of enjoyment from doing amateur events. When you're at an event like the Maratona dles Dolomites in Italy, or the Leadville 100 in Colorado, it's amazing to be a part of so many different types of people from all walks of life, enjoying their bikes and the thrill of riding.

I'm nearing the end of my career now and I'm enjoying it while I can, and maybe I feel more like that teenage fan who started off this whole adventure. After the mountain finishes at the Grand Tours, I try to take it all in because it's such a surreal thing to be a part of. We'll be riding back down to the buses, 190 guys all strung out in little groups, chatting to our friends, in the middle of this huge mess of fans and flags and families sitting outside of camper vans, and it will hit me, 'What the hell is this?' The crazy background scenes, the locations, the way we race full gas, like our lives depend on it, and then right after we can turn off and smile while we freewheel down a mountain. There's nothing else like it in the world.

ROGUE RIDERS

A rogue rider is every team manager's worst nightmare. Most of the time, they manage to cover it up so that the fans and the media don't get wind of any trouble, but arguments between teammates, and between riders and their sporting directors, are very common. Sometimes, if you're in a breakaway with someone, they'll just start screaming into the radio at the DS when they don't like what they've been told, or they might just pull the earpiece out and ignore their orders completely. More often than not, they're cutting off their nose to spite their face. Very few guys in the bunch like being told what to do, but most of us do it, knowing that the DS is experienced and ultimately wants what's best for us and the team. Occasionally though, you'll hear a rider lose his temper with the DS just because he reminds him to keep eating and drinking, and then towards the end of the stage, he's off the back because he bonked.

If a rider is talented enough, the team will more often than not choose to ignore the odd declaration of independence. Look at Chris Froome's infamous attack to La Toussuire in the 2012 Tour de France when Bradley Wiggins was in yellow. Froome ended up getting back into line and at the finish all the talk from the Sky riders was about a simple misunderstanding, but anyone with any understanding of bike racing could see what had happened. In that instance, Dave Brailsford brushed off talk about internal conflict and protected both riders, because he wanted Wiggins for that Tour and Froome for the future. If it had been a lesser rider, he'd have most likely been hung out to dry.

It's not just on the bike where riders can go rogue. There was also a strange case with Team LottoNL–Jumbo, when Juan José Lobato, Antwan Tolhoek, and Pascal Eenkhoorn were taken to the hospital during a December training camp in Spain because they couldn't be woken up. They'd taken unauthorised sleep aids. Lobato was fired, which is harsh, because I know he was going through a lot in his personal life at the time. But in fairness to the team, at twenty-nine, he should really know better. Eenkhoorn and Tolhoek were both suspended, probably because at twenty and twenty-three respectively, the management chalked it up to immaturity rather than inoperable stupidity.

It was a positive move from the team, in my opinion, because in the past, this kind of thing was just covered up and dealt with internally. There'd be a meeting, the riders involved would get a slap on the wrist and maybe a bit of a public dressing down in front of their teammates, but nothing would really happen, and they'd just do it again at the next camp. Firing the Spaniard and suspending the two Dutch kids sends a strong message to the rest of the squad, which is good, because I know a lot of the guys on that team and they're serious professionals and won't want to be working in that kind of environment. If you can't pull yourself together and behave properly at a training camp, you've no business being on the team. In the old days, if you found a teammate who was the worse for wear wandering around the hotel, you'd just keep it quiet and put him to bed, but it was always the same guys, because they never learned their lesson.

Riders who abuse sleeping pills do it because it can give you a powerful high, but you don't have a hangover. It was never my thing, because if I want to blow off some steam, I like wine and beer. And the hangover keeps you honest. You can't exaggerate all the time if you want to get up and train hard. But particularly the younger guys sometimes feel trapped because this is an ascetic lifestyle, you're not allowed to do an awful lot. It used to be common to use, and abuse, Stilnoct, a branded form of the drug zolpidem, which is also used in Ambien. It's meant as a short-term aid for people with insomnia but I definitely knew guys who were hooked on it. It's psycho-active and highly addictive, and I remember looking it up online and seeing reports of people doing some crazy things after taking it because sleepwalking is quite a common side-effect. There was one famous Belgian who I used to room with, and he'd go door to door at the races, to all of the riders he knew with sleeping tablets and ask them for one or two pills to help him sleep, but because he'd ask several different guys, he'd come back to the room with a handful. He was a sweet person and you couldn't say no to him, but in hindsight, we should have, because he clearly had a problem. One time we were away at a race, and I was dying with the flu, I couldn't breathe at all. I went to see the doctor and got a prescription for some medication, and just before I went down to the pharmacy he took it from me, and with a pencil, added some extra stuff for himself to the order. I was too young to appreciate just how serious that kind of behaviour really is, but the funny (or depressing) thing is, when I told that story to other riders, a lot of them had had the same experience. Apparently, it was pretty common.

In terms of contract disputes, one of the biggest ones in recent memory must have been Warren Barguil and Team Sunweb in 2017. It's always hard to know what's going on unless you're really close to the situation, but from what I hear from friends, there was nothing really malicious behind what Barguil did at the Vuelta when he rode away from his team-mate Wilco Kelderman, who had punctured during the seventh stage. He just didn't want to wait. In fairness to Warren, the general classification was close and he was thinking of his own result, but as a result Kelderman lost a lot of time and dropped down the GC. I think Warren had already waited once or twice earlier in the race, so maybe he didn't feel like Wilco had appreciated it enough. It's hard to know when you're looking in from the outside, but they never seemed overly close. Professional cyclists are a funny bunch, and we're used to being selfish, so something small like saying 'thanks' can make a huge difference. Whenever you talk to people close to the big champions, the one thing they all have in common is that they take very good care of those closest to them. When they win, their teammates feel like they win, too.

Barguil obviously wanted more respect from the team, or at least the right to ride for himself in the mountains, as he had done at the Tour earlier in the summer. I know a few guys on Sunweb though, and that's a team where the management has a very clear idea about how it wants to do things. Their plan for the Vuelta was to support Kelderman as the main GC rider, and regardless of how good Barguil was going, they weren't going to change that with a couple of weeks of racing still to go. I'm still not sure if kicking him out of the race was the best call to make, but I have to give them credit for making their decision quickly and not second-guessing it, because it takes balls to send home the reigning Tour de France King of the Mountains.

Given the fact that everyone knew he was leaving the team, that call was undoubtedly easier. They're backing Kelderman for the long haul, so while it would have been nice to get a couple of stage wins with Barguil, it ultimately wouldn't do much for the team's future plans. Showing that they're 100 per cent behind Wilco will boost the Dutchman's confidence. Seeing him in the bunch afterwards, he looked like a happier person, more relaxed and more chatty and smiling with his teammates. And he finished fourth, which when you look at the riders who finished ahead of him, is a very good result for a twenty-six-year-old. Chris Froome and Vincenzo Nibali are two of the most successful riders of all time and even Ilnur Zakarin, who came in third, is a reliable performer with a good palmarès, including stages at the Tour and the Giro and the overall win at the 2015 Tour de Romandie.

I heard that Warren had already told his teammates that he would leave Sunweb during the Tour de France in 2017, just after he won the stage from Saint-Girons to Foix. He still had a contract, so to the outside world it probably looked like a strange move. But I can understand his thinking. If he's not going to be a leader there, he needed to make a change. That team has some exciting young GC talent: Tom Dumoulin, Wilco Kelderman, and an exciting Dutch kid called Sam Oomen. When you meet Warren, it's clear pretty quickly that he believes in his own talents and that he sees himself at the very top of the sport, and looking at what he did at that Tour, you'd have to say he's right to think that way.

After the 2017 Giro d'Italia, Dumoulin was obviously the main man at Sunweb, so Barguil would have been fighting with Kelderman for leftovers. It was ironic that the team allowed him to find a new team, right before he won two stages in the Tour though. That proved his point somewhat, he clearly has a lot of ability and it probably made the bosses doubt themselves a little, but I can see their point of view too. Barguil is definitely capable of great things, but he's inconsistent and would have been on a big salary. The attraction is still obvious: Warren has been a huge name in France since his amateur days. I think he finished fifth at the 2011 Tour de l'Avenir, cycling's most prestigious U-jt23 race, when he was still a teenager ahead of some really big talents. He won it the next year, taking the points and the mountains jerseys as well. His first year as a pro, he won two stages at the Vuelta and the next year he went back to Spain and finished eighth overall, all before his twenty-third birthday. That's good going, and it made a big splash in the beginning, but since then he hasn't done enough to justify a big contract. Three and a half years without a win is a long time if you're asking for something like half a million euros.

This is a team sport, even if we forget it sometimes. And if you're selfish with the ball in football, the coach isn't going to pick you unless you're Cristiano Ronaldo or Lionel Messi. You play your role in the team, or you're on the bench. It's a rare decision to see in cycling, but if I was in the same position as the managers, I'd send him home as well. You can't have a guy going rogue without being punished if you're constantly telling everyone else to do as they're told and follow the plan. There would be chaos.

They did something similar with Marcel Kittel, when they let him out of his deal a year early so that he could join Etixx–Quick-Step, and that's a much bigger loss to any team because at the time he was the world's best sprinter. It just looks like a team that doesn't want to let fame or egos get in the way. Kittel is a good guy and you know he's going to deliver big wins every year, but they won the Giro d'Italia in 2017 and if they had to keep paying his big salary and building a lead-out train for his sprints, I'm not sure they'd have been able to achieve that. Sunweb's CEO, Iwan Spekenbrink, was open about the move in the press, which I liked. I wish more teams were open like that. Warren apparently went to them looking for a move, and after they had a think about it, they gave him his wish. My guess would be that they didn't want an unhappy rider on the team the following season, and also, given that he's rumoured to be on around €500,000 per year, it would have given them some more money to play with while planning for their next big goals.

After the 2018 Tour, I was expecting Geraint Thomas to go rogue, to be honest. He's only got a few more good years left in him, and even with a Tour win under his belt, it's hard to see him getting free rein at Team Sky. Froome is one of the most successful riders of all time, so he will still be calling the shots. Even when Thomas was clearly the stronger rider in 2018, they were still backing Froome more than the Welshman, which must have stung. He handled it well, but if I'd been in the same position, I wouldn't have been happy. For example, Froome was the only protected rider for the team time trial, so even though Thomas was leading his teammate by fifty-two seconds at that point, if he'd had a puncture or crashed, the others wouldn't have waited for him and his race would have been over. I also read that in one of the hotels they stayed in, the shoddy electrics kept tripping because of all the air conditioners, so the team management declared that Froome was the only rider allowed to turn his on. Thomas is a cool character, but if he'd thrown his toys out of the pram after the Tour because of all that, I don't think many riders in the peloton would have blamed him.

Another concern for him has to be the young Colombian rider, Egan Bernal. He was sensational in 2018, and he was still only twenty-one. Sky have signed him up to a five-year contract, which is almost unheard of in cycling, so Dave Brailsford clearly sees him as the future of the team. I get why Thomas stayed, he's been part of that setup his whole career and even with all the competition it's probably the best place for him, but it's hard to see him getting too many chances when he's vying for primacy with a six-time Grand Tour champion and arguably the brightest young talent in the sport.

TEAM SKY

This might sound surprising coming from someone who has been around as long as I have, but seeing Team Sky involved in so much controversy over the last couple of years has been really upsetting. Bradley Wiggins had always been something of a hero to me, and then the stories came out about mysterious deliveries in Jiffy bags.

For anyone who miraculously managed to miss the shitshow that surrounded this issue for the last couple of years, let me recap.

In autumn 2016, a group of Russian hackers known as the Fancy Bears released documents that showed Wiggins had been given permission, something known as a therapeutic use exemption (TUE), to use the banned corticosteroid triamcinolone before all of his biggest races in 2011, 2012 and 2013, including the 2012 Tour de France, which he won. This was followed by a lengthy investigation by the UK Anti-Doping Agency (UKAD) into a package – the Jiffy bag, which allegedly also contained triamcinolone – that had been delivered to Team Sky during the Critérium du Dauphiné in 2011. Just like he'd do the following July at the Tour, Wiggins went on to win that Dauphiné. Thanks to some missing medical records, UKAD had to drop the case, but an inquiry in the British parliament was running concurrently and it agreed with much of UKAD's assumptions, claiming that Team Sky had gamed the rules by abusing the TUE system and that they had 'crossed an ethical line'. It seems clear that the abuse was a regular occurrence, but the Jiffy bag caught the public eye, partly because the scandal had a catchy name, I'm sure, but also because no one at Team Sky, the self-professed masters of micro-management in the pursuit of marginal gains, could remember exactly what happened and none of them thought to make a note of it.

Stay with me. According to Team Sky, Wiggins' team at the time, the Jiffy bag contained Fluimucil, a decongestant that you can buy over the counter across Europe for pocket change. UKAD were adamant that Sky's files showed no record of any Fluimucil purchase. There were, however, plenty of receipts for triamcinolone. Even allowing for a missing receipt, though, there was still the reasonable question: why send someone on a flight with something you could just get in a pharmacy?

Without joining Sky as a spy, there's no way I can say for sure what's going on there, but reading reports about them ordering fifty-five vials of the corticosteroid triamcinolone between 2010 and 2013, or buying Fluimucil for Bradley Wiggins from a pharmacy in Switzerland because it wasn't licensed for use in the UK, you have to wonder. That's just human nature. Wiggins and Sky strongly refute any claims that triamcinolone was ever used to enhance performance, but I've ridden for several teams with differing ethical codes over the years, and I have never known a team doctor that would do something like that. Fluimucil is just a harmless drug that helps clear mucus from lungs and it's not on WADA's prohibited list, but it comes with a strong warning against its use if you suffer from asthma, which Wiggins does, and there are easy alternatives that Sky could have bought in any British pharmacy. They could definitely have handled it better by being more transparent, but I think the team has changed a lot since Brailsford launched it in 2010.

Sky said that Simon Cope, a former pro cyclist who worked as a coach for British Cycling and now works for Team Wiggins, picked up the Jiffy bag in Manchester and flew it to Geneva, from where he drove to France to meet the team. His expenses showed that he had actually made a lengthy journey to Sussex – a round trip of about 900 kilometres – to pick up the package before his flight, but when he was questioned about this by MPs, he laughed it off, suggesting he was just trying to 'fiddle' expenses. Once he got to France, he handed it off to Dr Richard Freeman, the team doctor, and headed home. Freeman was called to give testimony before the parliamentary committee, but he was excused on medical grounds. Which was unfortunate for anyone who was hoping to get to the bottom of this story, because when all other excuses failed, Team Sky eventually pinned the blame on him, saying that the relevant files had been on his computer, which he lost while on holiday in Greece.

UKAD apparently followed up the laptop claim with Interpol, but we never heard any more of it, and while there was some threat made at the time that he might be brought up before the British General Medical Council to account for his woeful record-keeping, I don't think that happened either. I'm not interested in one man taking the fall for Sky though, because I know from experience that there would have to have been a lot of people involved in that process. Of course, it all might be true. Truth can be stranger than fiction, and I know some people working in this sport that might just be incompetent enough to string together a list of unfortunate events like that, but this is supposedly the best-run team in cycling, spending big money flying cheap, over-the-counter drugs around Europe for no good reason while also leaving important medical files offline and on laptops that get lost by the beach somewhere. Between the mystery packages, the changing stories, the TUEs, and the timely thefts, my honest reaction was quite simply, 'What the fuck?'

I was really angry. I always liked Wiggins as a person, he's a good guy to talk to and I thought he was cool, a little bit eccentric, and always outspoken. When he won the Tour de France in 2012 I was genuinely happy for him and for cycling, because I thought he was a good, clean winner.

Now we know that they were doing a lot of the corticosteroid triamcinolone. It's sad. When Sky first came to the peloton, they were supposed to be whiter than white, and instead, they're a very dark shade of grey, and involved in a lot of murky business that a really clean team would steer well clear of. OK, there's a line, and until you've crossed it, you haven't broken any rules, but my team tries to keep a few metres back from that precipice because if you're constantly walking the edge, it's easy to fall over.

You can call that gaming the system if you like, but for me, any time you exploit a loophole, hoping to gain an advantage on the rest of the bunch, you're in the wrong. Maybe the rulebook says otherwise, and in the cut-throat world of professional sports, perhaps it's smart to use every tool at your disposal in order to win, but personally, I think that most people know when they're doing something that's wrong, regardless of what the exact legal boundaries are. I used to think a lot of Team Sky and I admired the values that they seemed to want to promote, but it's not like that any more. Like a lot of cycling fans around the world, I feel disappointed and a little betrayed. They were supposed to be the clean future of cycling, and now all they're doing is tarnishing the already-battered reputation of the sport I love.

Wiggins says that triamcinolone, something that we all know is performance enhancing, was absolutely needed to help treat his hay fever. It seems excessive, but I'd be willing to give a rider whom I admired the benefit of the doubt, if it hadn't been so obvious that Sky were abusing the TUE system to get the upper hand. Wiggins' old coach Shane Sutton admitted as much to a BBC documentary at the end of 2017, saying that at Sky, TUEs were seen as just another tool to be used in the pursuit of those mythical 'marginal gains', something that could add the final touches to an athlete's conditioning before a big event without breaking any anti-doping rules.

In Sutton's own words: 'If you've got an athlete that's 95 per cent ready and that little 5 per cent niggle or injury that's troubling them, if you can get the TUE to get them to 100 per cent, of course you would. The business you're in is to give you the edge on your opponent and ultimately it's about killing them off but you definitely don't cross the line and that's something we've never done.'

For a team that's supposed to have a zero-tolerance approach to cheating, that's a pretty nonchalant attitude to the ethics of sport. And as someone who's been competing against them, and who has had to fight really hard to show people that I'm clean rather than being able to hide behind Team Sky's innocent image and clever marketing, it makes me want to scream.

UK Anti-Doping had to close its inquiry into the contents of the surreptitious package because despite a lengthy investigation and the best efforts of a lot of good people, it wasn't able to find a smoking gun, the irrefutable evidence that could either exonerate or incriminate those involved definitively. And that's a shame, because we can't lift the suspicion that all this has attached to Wiggins.

For his part, Bradley continues to deny any wrongdoing, which is fair enough, but he has no right to call it a 'malicious witch hunt'. This is a guy who railed against the dopers during the EPO era, and who was so incensed after being kicked off the 2007 Tour de France, thanks to his Cofidis teammate Cristian Moreni's positive test, that he threw his team kit in the bin at Pau airport and vowed to never be seen wearing it again. When the TUE scandal broke, he could have cleared it all up by providing medical documentation and a sound explanation. He did neither, instead preferring to dodge questions and hide behind his clean record – in the same way as every doper he ever hated.

Losing medical records is something I can't get my head around. This is a team that brings a mattress and anti-allergen pillows for every rider, in case they pick up a bug from the hotel bedding. Handshakes are banned at races, and there's even a video teaching staff and riders the 'right' way to wash their hands. Sir Dave Brailsford is famously pedantic about the minutiae of life within Team Sky, and the team doctors are, well, doctors. Detailed records are an essential part of the medical profession, and while Sky can claim all they want that the nature of elite-level competition made it difficult to keep an account of everything, I'm pretty sure you could say that the nature of an emergency room in a busy hospital makes it hard to keep documentation too. But they have to do it anyway.

Some people are willing to accept the fact that Richard Freeman, the doctor at the centre of the Wiggins scandal, had a lot of riders to treat and that he just forgot to make a note of some things, but would they take that excuse from a doctor in their own life? I don't think so.

And they can say that there's nothing wrong with using corticosteroids, that it was a valid solution to Bradley's condition, but I think that's nonsense. For one thing, I know it wouldn't be allowed on my squad. I've always been with teams that were members of the *Mouvement Pour un Cyclisme Crédible*, the MPCC, which is an organisation that aims to defend the idea of a clean cycling based on notions of transparency and responsibility. For an MPCC team, an eight-day exclusion from racing is required for any rider who needs corticoid treatment, regardless of the fact that a TUE allows them to show up at the start line. The thinking goes that anyone who's ill enough to need an emergency injection isn't well enough to race. In 2014, Chris Horner couldn't defend his Vuelta a España title for that reason, and if Sky had been in the MPCC in 2012, Brad Wiggins would never have been a part of the nine-man Sky squad that began the ninety-ninth Tour de France in the Belgian city of Liège.

Corticosteroids had a place in the old way of cycling, but it's a long time since they've been an acceptable option. You can read all about it in Thomas Dekker's book, for example, when he talks about not being allowed to use cortisone at Rabobank back in 2008. That's a serial doper on a dirty team, a decade ago, in what everyone knows as the dirtiest period for the sport. And five years later, Wiggins is still using it? It's total bullshit. David Millar said that triamcinolone was the most powerful drug that he ever used – including the erythropoietin that eventually got him banned!

So it's more potent than EPO, and yet a doctor at Sky thought it was fine for the team's star rider to take it via intramuscular injection, to treat hay fever.

It's been banned for such a long time that I can't understand anyone who's involved in elite sport suggesting that it's OK to use. I've only had a couple of corticosteroid injections in my life, both on my knee when I was younger, and I'm happy about that because I think it has serious side-effects, too. It can cause insomnia, mood swings, high blood pressure, ulcers, thin skin, and it can really affect your bone density, so it's common to hear rumours in the peloton about anyone who breaks a lot of bones. And while I'm not a doctor, I don't think adding a hormone to a body that doesn't need it can be a good thing, long term.

Looking back on it now, even though I wasn't allowed to race for eight days after the injection, I did a really good race after that break, I don't know if the corticosteroids helped in that regard, but it certainly didn't hurt my form that weekend, even though I had been out injured for a month or so. Then, after pushing it for a few days racing, the pain came back, and we decided to try something else. In the end, a good chiropractor did a much better job of curing the problem.

Using cortisone used to be normal, but by the time I was joining the pro ranks it was already considered dodgy. I actually remember being offered an injection by a team doctor on another occasion, because I was really congested and he said it would help, but it would have gone in my book, which at the time was how you kept a record of any serious medication. I knew that there was a performance-enhancing element to it and that it might, one day, be questioned, so I said no. Anyway, it was a flat course, set up for a bunch sprint, so as a skinny little climber, I had no chance. 'Don't worry about it, Doc, I don't need it,' I said. 'I'm not going to win anyway, so I can lose with a blocked nose.'

As for Sky, they did nothing to break the actual rules. I personally think they made a mockery out of the spirit of the rules, but by the letter of the law they've done nothing wrong, based on what we know today. They applied to the UCI for a TUE, which was issued according to guidelines set out by the World Anti-Doping Agency, WADA. And perhaps the hay fever showing up on the eve of each season's biggest objective was coincidental. But given that the sport's most organised and efficient outfit could lose the medical records pertaining to the TUEs in question, and the fact that Wiggins himself claimed, in his 2012 autobiography *My Time*, to have never had an injection for anything more than some hospital drips and immunisation shots, one has to wonder. But listening to the Sky defence, it was like they didn't realise what they were saying, admitting to using it as a way to gain an edge on a rival. That's cheating, plain and simple. Now I can understand why Sky never joined the MPCC.

It's also disappointing from a personal perspective, because I was going for general classifications, too, and we never could seem to get as skinny as those guys. I like to think of myself as a really professional guy, I take my diet and training really seriously and I'm always very lean, but showing up to the start of one of the Grand Tours, the Sky riders always appeared to be able to take it to the next level. Then, when you understand more about how corticosteroids work, you know that you can get skinny pretty easy, without getting sick. So I was there, pushing my body to the limit and doing everything I could to arrive to the Giro d'Italia or the Tour de France in top shape, and meanwhile they were going past those limits with the help of drugs. Legally, it's a grey area, but for me it's so grey that it's almost black. It's a dark part of sport that I don't think any honest athlete would want to visit, and I'm happy that I'm not a Team Sky rider right now because if I was I'd be ashamed.

That said, I don't think everyone else's reputation there should be subject to the same suspicion as Wiggins. There are a lot of talented athletes there that don't deserve to suffer by association. For example, the only time Chris Froome's name is mentioned in the entire 56 pages of the parliamentary report was in a footnote relating to an interview that he gave in 2016, questioning Wiggins' use of TUEs, as reported by the *Guardian*. In my experience, he's a hardworking guy, softly spoken, a model professional. He doesn't look particularly elegant on a bike, but I've been really impressed with a few of his victories in recent years. You still hear criticism about him being robotic, but it's not fair any more. Sure, he likes to stare at the power meter and in interviews he doesn't come across as very passionate or intriguing, but on the bike, he's developed a real flair for attacking and he knows how to light up a race. I respect him for that.

If I was him, I'd be really pissed at how Sky handled his salbutamol issue in 2018. Transparency would have helped a lot, and avoided Froome's reputation taking unnecessary abuse from fans and media who were quick to make an unmerited connection to the Wiggins case. Froome's urine sample at the 2017 Vuelta a España showed excessive levels of salbutamol but after months of handwringing and debate in the papers, the UCI and WADA eventually agreed that it didn't constitute an Adverse Analytical Finding and that there had been no wrongdoing on Froome's part. There are several things that could have produced a spike in the reading – WADA's own press release on the matter cited "illness, use of medication, chronic use of salbutamol at varying doses over the course of weeks of high intensity competition". These things can and do happen. Our bodies go through incredible stresses during a Grand Tour and testing anomalies are not uncommon. What I can't understand though is why Sky or the UCI haven't released more details about it.

While most people were focused on Froome, my major issues were with the UCI. I know how many things can affect the tests and I can only imagine how difficult it must be to deal with all of the criticism in the press while you're fighting to prove your innocence. But the fact that the UCI took so long to sort the whole mess out was ridiculous, and their unwillingness to be fully transparent makes a rod for the sport's back. Even when riders are proven innocent, like Froome, doubts remain among a section of fans, journalists, and riders.

One criticism that I have to aim at Froome is this: I didn't like his statements about asthma on Twitter, because it felt like he was attempting to use the public's sympathy for asthma sufferers to distract from the issue. He wrote:

'It's sad seeing the misconceptions that are out there about athletes & salbutamol use. My hope is that this doesn't prevent asthmatic athletes from using their inhalers in emergency situations for fear of being judged. It is not something to be ashamed of.'

I suffer from exercise-induced asthma, or rather, from exercise-induced bronchoconstriction, the condition's proper name, because exercise doesn't actually cause the asthma, it's just a trigger. A lot of you probably have it to, but unless you're pushing your body to its limits, you could go your whole life without realising it. There are a lot of things that you don't have to worry about unless you're a professional athlete, for instance, is one of your feet bigger than the other? Probably, but not enough to affect your daily life. It's common for pros in a lot of sports to get custom-made shoes though. Or how about your legs? Most of us are asymmetrical, but again, it's not really an issue. When Marco Pantani was making his remarkable comeback after a bad accident in the 1995 Milano–Torino, even after he overcame the worst of it, one of the big remaining worries was that the crash had shortened his left leg by several millimetres and there were serious doubts about the effect that would have on his performance.

As for asthma, lots of athletes have it, and let me tell you: no one is ashamed of it. It's totally normal, easily treatable, and these days, no barrier to being successful. The British long-distance runner Paula Radcliffe won an abundance of medals and set the world record time for a marathon with asthma, and the Manchester United legend Paul Scholes didn't let it stop him playing an integral part in eleven Premier League title wins or two Champions League triumphs. I don't know the exact number of riders in the peloton today with some form of asthma, but from talking to the team doctor about my own symptoms, it's probably something like one in five. Even Vincenzo Nibali, who Froome beat to win the 2017 Vuelta, has it. I understand that Froome must have felt under attack unfairly, but I didn't like the way his statements made it sound like the debate surrounding his personal result in a standard-ised test that we all take was a general attack on people with asthma. As professional athletes we're in the public eye and we have to accept that we're under scrutiny. I'm sure it was unpleasant, but there was uncertainty about the case for a time and in a sport like ours, you have to expect that people will be suspicious until you're proved innocent, as Froome has been. If I was him, rather than complaining about people questioning his use of asthma medication, I'd have been complaining about how long it was taking the UCI to confirm my innocence.

THE MEDIA

Most professional athletes are wary – and probably weary – of the press and of the fans. It's not that we don't want to be open, it's just that nowadays all it takes is a misinterpreted remark or an ill-considered phrase to ruin a career, so it can be really difficult to strike the right balance when you're dealing with the media. I'm a fan of cycling too, and I still love reading about the sport and listening to the commentary. But the press corps these days is completely unrecognisable compared to fifteen or twenty years ago. For one, there's a twenty-four-hour news cycle, and so many websites that are all hungry for content. Constantly. On top of that, you've got fan forums and Twitter, so rumours and gossip can spread like wildfire. There's a huge range in terms of quality, too. Unless I'm totally cooked after a stage, or I've had a crash, I'm happy to stop and chat with someone if they genuinely need something or if we have a relationship, but a lot of times it just feels like they're there on the finish line just for the sake of it, or maybe it's to be seen.

For the teams, the media is vital, because without coverage, there would be no sponsors. But these days it's all about controlling the narrative. The team want attention, but for the most part, only when it suits them. Different teams have contrasting approaches to the press, for instance, the smaller Italian, French, or Spanish teams will do whatever they can to get some column inches because that's what their sponsors are paying for. They're not going to win the big races, so they have to be friendly or interesting in different ways. They usually have good relationships with the journalists and are happy to give them a ride or organise an interview. Jonathan Vaughters' teams are good with the media as well, even though they're one of the 'bigger' names, and the Mitchelton–Scott guys do a brilliant job of creating their own content in-house, like videos on the bus or of the guys out training.

I've been on teams that paid close attention to what was being said about them, and I've been on teams where everyone was more relaxed about it. In general, I think the latter is a better approach, because if you're too sensitive or you react strongly to every little criticism, it's going to rub some journalists up the wrong way, and they'll just be waiting to stick the knife in when you mess up. The management here is open to the media and the atmosphere is usually pretty good, we make sure that we don't ignore reporters and in turn they're usually fair when something has gone wrong in a race. It's still possible for the most powerful newspapers to exert some influence on the sport, particularly in cycling's heartland in continental Europe, and a journalist can still write somebody out of a job.

They've always been good to me and I try to be good in return. I have a huge collection of cycling books, and when I was a kid I bought everything that I could get my hands on. Now, there's so much coming out, I can't read everything, not least because I'm a professional athlete who has a young family, but I still try to get the best stuff and I'm always swapping recommendations with other riders. The gossip and the silly stuff online is a waste of time, but the best writing, that's also a huge part of cycling for me. In the early days of my career, whenever I was abroad on a training camp or at a race, I'd be delighted to find a sports newspaper from back home in a local shop. It was probably a day or two old, but I'd smile the whole way back to the hotel because I was looking forward to reading my favourite columnists and seeing what was happening elsewhere in the cycling world. Now you can lose yourself online reading for hours. It's not as romantic as it once was, but there's so much variety and I think there's still a lot of excellent writing that comes from cycling. This is a sport in which great stories are born and I think the literature plays a big part in cycling's enduring popularity. It's part of the magic.

At the same time, it's a pain in the arse when some guy is knocking on your hotel door on the rest day of a Grand Tour. And once they get your phone number, it can be a nightmare. I'm friendly with some journalists, and I'll try to respond, but we need our own personal time away from racing as well. It pisses me off when someone comes to me with a question about another team, or some rider I barely know, or what my team is doing for 'marginal gains'. That's not even a real thing, it's just some marketing bullshit that Team Sky made up to make themselves sound clever. The stupid questions can really get under your skin, because it could be the middle of a three-week race and I'm in some miserable hotel room, exhausted, probably in some sort of pain, I haven't seen my family for weeks, or even been able to do something basic like sit on the couch and have a beer, and this guy is asking me about marginal gains. I feel like saying, 'Do your fucking job properly and leave me alone', but I can't. What do they want me to say? Do they think I'm stupid enough to accuse Team Sky or anyone else for that matter of doing something when I don't know for sure? My team manager and my sponsors would love that. Or are they that stupid that they still believe that marginal gains are a thing and that I should be thinking up cute little ways to get some advantage. Maybe we should go back to the 1960s and start drilling holes in the cranks and the brake levers to save a couple of grams. Is that marginal enough?

I'm curious to know what's happening at the other teams too. I genuinely think that the majority of the peloton is doing things the right way these days, but there will always be some scumbag trying to exploit the system, so rather than bothering me when I'm trying to get some rest, those guys should be off doing some actual reporting and investigating whoever they think looks suspicious. At the Tour de France in 2017, I was getting questions about Brad Wiggins and his therapeutic use exemptions, or about the fact that Sky had been sent a bunch of testosterone patches, and I had nothing to do with it! They want some other fool to go on record complaining about this or that and making accusations, rather than actually doing the hard work to find out if something illegal actually happened. That's their job, rather than just being a fan boy and re-printing press releases. I think Paul Kimmage is the only one who's been questioning Sky from the start, for example. Everyone else just took Sky's version, hook, line, and sinker. It makes me laugh when I read people saying that Paul's just angry or bitter, because I'd be bitter too if I went through what he did. And we shouldn't forget that he's been right about everything else.

More of the teams now want to be like football teams, totally removed from the fans and the journalists. They have ropes up around the bus, and the press officer deals with everything. Riders aren't allowed to have a conversation with someone in the media without the press guy sticking his nose in. And they control all the data. There's tonnes of it that's readily available, and for some reason they want to hide it. Why not have it all on Strava or something similar so that everyone can see just how hard we work? To me it seems like those teams are terrified of someone having an opinion about them that doesn't match up with their brand book or their marketing strategy. They're so self-conscious, but in my experience, it's best for your mental health if you just accept it as a fact of life and try to roll with the punches. Not everyone is going to like you, even if you're the nicest guy in the world or the cleanest, fairest team in the peloton. You can either ignore it, or accept the criticism, but unless it's something totally outlandish and you have to defend yourself for the sake of your contract or your reputation, it's better not to fight it. I remember coming back from a race and we were all in the airport waiting for the flight. Our team leader had retired from the race after a horrible crash, a really high-speed, high-impact collision. He looked like he'd been thrown out of a car at eighty kilometres per hour. And as we sat there, the sports round-up came on the TV and the commentators just savaged us, saying that we were all useless and that he didn't deserve to be leading such a big team. That was rough because we couldn't just turn it off, and for a while afterwards I know it had an effect on him. It wasn't true, we all knew that there was nothing he could have done to avoid the fall, racing is just like that sometimes, but it still hurt.

In the past, I've been totally open with some journalists who had questions about my past and my performance levels, and when they came to me, I felt like the best response was to answer truthfully and show them whatever they wanted to see, so they looked at my training logs and my biological passport data, one guy even had an independent expert look at it, but there was nothing dubious and we all moved on. I'm not sure if it ever even ended up in the newspaper, because there was no story. Perhaps other riders would say no or view that as an invasion of privacy, but at the time I felt like all these people were being caught doping, and even more were being publicly accused without any evidence, so when they came to me, I just said, 'OK, have a look.' To me, there was no harm in it because I trusted them, I'd known them for a while, and I felt like the best way of keeping my name out of the mud was to be as open as possible. And when you look at the mess other riders have caused for themselves simply by being difficult or withdrawn, I stand by my decision.

Having had that conversation with my friends, I can see how it might help in some situations. For example, if a rider doesn't know he's going to be at a race but he gets called up late for whatever reason, you could look back at his training schedule and take a good guess at what kind of form he'll be in. Of course, he could always be bluffing, and not uploading all his rides. For me personally, there's no legitimate reason not to share those files, especially if you want to keep the rumours at bay. Maybe I won't put everything up because I forget or whatever, but on the whole I think it's good for the fans to see. I understand that some people like their privacy, but when the gossip starts to circulate, sharing is the best way to shut it down. Sunlight is the best disinfectant, and I don't think Romain Bardet is losing any sleep, desperately wishing he could see what kind of hill repeats Chris Froome likes to do in the off-season. Files from big races is a different thing. I don't mind sharing them because my approach is very straight-forward – I just go as hard as I can until my director tells me to stop. But I can understand why a big time-trial star like Tony Martin or Tom Dumoulin would want to keep that stuff to themselves, because if you know how to read the values properly, it can reveal a lot about their technique and their approach.

Not everyone is comfortable with total transparency, which is a shame, but it's also the duty of the press to convince them. I know a lot of good people in the bunch who have been fucked over by reporters, either they were misquoted, quoted out of context, or their name was attached to some gossip without any basis. That kind of thing can cause real problems for a rider, not just within his team or with sponsors, but at home, too. I know my wife would be furious if she started seeing my name linked to doping allegations or some race-fixing scandal. And I wouldn't like my kids to grow up and then find some old bullshit article about me online that wasn't true. With good journalists, it's different, because the relationship is developed over time and is built on trust. It just takes work, and not all journalists or athletes are willing to make the effort.

That's not *omertà*. *Omertà* is about covering up illegal activities, but sometimes a lazy journalist will use it as a buzzword whenever a rider or a team isn't as open to questioning as they would like. I've been on teams that liked to be more closed off, and I've ridden with great riders who didn't like talking publicly. I always respected that, and did my own thing, being careful to never disrespect a teammate or a manager because the story is never just about me. This is a team sport, and what I say has an effect on the guys around me. It's not fair for someone to say something in a team meeting or in the hotel room, and then see it the next week in an article somewhere. It doesn't even have to be anything shocking or scandalous; some people just like to keep their opinions and their personal situations private and it's important to respect that.

As a rookie, I saw things that I should have reported, things that I would report now. It's your entire livelihood on the line though, and for a kid of twenty or twenty-one, that's an impossibly hard call to make. I also don't think it should be up to them. I would be incredibly impressed with someone if they came out and exposed something illicit in their team because I believe in clean sport, but riders shouldn't be expected to police the sport because they're too close to it. When I was that age, there was no incentive to do it, I hope that's changed now, but back then? The only precedent was Christophe Bassons, this lovely, honest kid who was bullied out of the peloton for daring to question the doping culture. The infamous conversation he had with Lance Armstrong, broadcast around

the world, in which the American wanted to show who was
boss by telling his troublesome French colleague to keep his
mouth shut, was bad enough. His own Française des Jeux team
turned on him too, however, and didn't give him a share of
their prize money. Teams always share prize money, it's a fundamental part of the operation. Cutting him out of it was an
elemental, unequivocal 'Fuck you.' It's different now, thankfully.
The culture has changed and there's more support, but it's still
not a totally black-and-white situation and I'd defend a rider
who knew about a teammate doing something wrong, because
it's such a complicated environment. We're all professional
athletes who've signed up to play by certain rules, but we're
also friends. Secrets are shared in confidence because there's
a bond there, and while the correct thing to do is blatantly
obvious, it's not so easy. If you knew your best friend was
having an affair, or cheating on their taxes, would you run to
tell their partner or the taxman? Maybe, or maybe not. Maybe
you'd tell them to stop being such a dickhead, and hope that
they change their ways.

DOPING

In my opinion cycling has a huge problem when it comes to terminology. I often think that when someone hears the word 'doping' they immediately think of the extreme stuff, like the blood bags and EPO in cycling, steroids in baseball, or maybe Ivan Drago getting pumped full of everything by a laboratory full of evil scientists in *Rocky IV*. The reality is totally different. Most, if not all, athletes use something that could be considered a performance-enhancing drug. It's a spectrum. When I started out as a pro, intravenous recovery was considered to be normal. Now, it's banned in cycling, but not in other sports.

So a cyclist isn't allowed to use any needles without a TUE. If they do, and they're caught, they're in trouble. But elsewhere, it's not a big deal. To give just one example, in 2017, the former Manchester United manager José Mourinho got into a very public spat with England's Football Association after finding out that his club's player, the defender Phil Jones, had been given six local anaesthetic injections in his thigh before a meaningless friendly match with Germany. Six! Jones's injury subsequently reappeared during the game and he hobbled off, and the debate in the press was about whether or not he should have been playing, rather than whether or not anyone should be sticking six needles into a professional athlete. The public perception is that football doesn't have a problem, despite overwhelming evidence to the contrary, so when FIFA's own chief medical officer, Dr Jiri Dvorak, declared a few years ago that, in his estimation, half of all international players were using painkillers as part of their pre-match routine, almost no one seemed to care. And when FIFA removed him from his position at the end of 2017, at the same time as he was investigating the possibility of a systematic abuse of performance-enhancing drugs in Russian football, few people thought it strange. Had the same thing happened in cycling, or track and field, there'd have been a media frenzy.

When I joined the pro ranks, the use of needles was still allowed. Banning their use was one of the best advancements in the sport in recent years, in my opinion, because when you're young and stupid, going from a vitamin shot to something stronger isn't that big a leap. It's all a needle, and it comes from the doctor. You've probably spent your entire adolescent life training and working towards being a professional, so it's normal to be totally myopic and not think too deeply about peripheral things. The doctor is an expert, with an expensive education and years of experience, and you're just a kid, so you go along with what he says. That, to me, is one of the great injustices of that era. There was such a betrayal of trust, of young athletes who trusted their superiors, and also of the parents who couldn't be there all the time. They were handing their babies over to these teams who had a duty of care and instead they were being corrupted. Anyway, one needle looked much the same as another, so walking into the hotel room to find your teammate with a syringe in his arm wasn't the surprise it should have been. Even when the bath is full of bloody towels because he made a mistake with the needle, it wasn't really shocking because it had been normalised.

It made me uncomfortable, but at least in my experience, the real line was crossed the first time that a doctor gave me a shot for recovery. That was a genuinely uneasy experience, because he just said it was good for you, and that was that. It wasn't a discussion. I was in a room full of other riders, and the doctor just walked around with a big vial filling up the needles and handing them to us so we co do it ourselves to save him time. One of the guys said, 'Imagine if our mums could see us doing this', and I suppose it made us laugh at the time, but it made me a little worried too because I knew that there was a deeper truth to the joke. I made peace with it afterwards, because it was part of the job and I trusted that there was nothing bad in it, and I know that a lot of doctors will say that that kind of recovery aid is healthier for athletes like us, pushing the limits, but I still think banning needles was the best thing for the sport because it sent a message. When it happened, back in 2011, there were guys up in arms, terrified that we wouldn't be able to finish a Grand Tour without that kind of medication, but we're fine without it. That gives you some idea of how far some riders had been sucked into those habits.

I knew some friends were using testosterone and things like that, but none of the really heavy stuff, that was too far up the food chain. It wasn't like they'd just come up to you at the start of a race and start listing off the drugs they were taking. For someone like me, it was almost an abstract thing, I knew it went on, but I didn't know much else because it never interested me. I wasn't the biggest rider, I was never a prolific winner as an amateur, and when I turned pro, it was already a huge victory for me. I was just happy to be getting paid for riding my bike. And aside from the moral issue, doping seemed so stressful. When you read about what they were up to now, hiding it in other people's homes, sneaking across the border, spying on other dopers to find out the latest and greatest drugs, it took a lot of work. I was already exhausted just from training.

It might be hard to believe for a fan, but a lot of riders in the bunch felt the same as I did. It's not that we weren't competitive or that we didn't want to succeed, it was that guys like me felt that they had won the lottery already and they just wanted to work hard, keep their heads down, and enjoy the ride. Every two years, I doubled my contract, I moved up the ladder in terms of races, and eventually got to do the biggest races like the Giro d'Italia and the Tour de France. I was riding my bike, having fun, and I didn't think about the other guys too much. There were always rumours, of course, some riders would leave the blinds closed all day so that the doping control inspectors couldn't see in, or crazy stories like the one about the Dutch rider Stefan van Dijk. Back in 2005, he saw the yellow anti-doping bus outside his house in Belgium and decided to just speed off rather than taking the test. Obviously, the doctor recognised him straight away and he was done for refusing a test.

Friendship and proximity is going to lead to some acquiescence. I know it shouldn't, in a perfect world, but I hope you can see what I mean when I say that it wasn't always a clear-cut choice. A rider's loyalty is going to be more with his friends than anyone else, it certainly wasn't with the UCI or the media, especially back in the day because it just seemed rigged to protect the big names and make sure the money kept flowing in for everyone. Right now, I'd certainly report it, but it's a different world. And if I'm being totally honest, it would be easier, because at my age, I have less to lose.

I have a problem with the riders who've since come out and blamed absolutely everything on dope. That's an issue I have with the media, because it can be weaponised by people with an agenda, and without meaning any disrespect to the majority of fans or journalists, very few of them really know what they're talking about when we discuss performance-enhancing drugs. When I read those guys moaning in a magazine feature or attacking people on social media, I wish I could just phone them up and personally say 'Fuck off.' They just weren't good enough. Look at the notorious dopers: Lance Armstrong started winning triathlons when he was thirteen and he was the road race world champion before his twenty-second birthday. Marco Pantani did the amateur Giro d'Italia three times before turning pro, and he finished third, second, and then first. Thomas Dekker had more talent as a kid than most seasoned pros could ever dream of. I raced with one well-known doper as an amateur – I won't say who because it might give too much away about my own identity – and he won twenty times as many races as I did before turning pro. The dope then made a difference, without a doubt, but it was a marginal gain, to borrow Dave Brailsford's favourite phrase. If you couldn't get near those guys, you just didn't have it. I consider myself to be a very good rider, I'd have to be to finish in the top ten at Grand Tours, but no amount of drugs would get me to that level. Just think of Joe Papp, the American pro turned journalist; he's more famous for helping the United States Anti-Doping Agency in their case against Floyd Landis than anything he did as a bike rider, and he took so many drugs that it almost killed him. The quantity of EPO and blood thinners in his body turned a routine, low-speed fall into a life-threatening ordeal in an Italian hospital.

A lot of guys are bitter about it. They wonder if they could have used EPO for a couple of years and then quit once they reached the top. These are riders who can't finish a stage race. Come on, if you don't have the engine, that's it. One of the best developments in recent years has been the kind of coaching we receive from an early age. If you go back twenty years, a lot of guys were over-training because they didn't really know what they were doing. We're not all built the same, and some guys need more rest than others. So you could have a real talent who could put out great numbers on a good day, but he couldn't hold it together over the course of a stage race or be consistent throughout the season. Take Greg Van Avermaet, he can train every day, 180 kilometres at 36 kilometres per hour in a big gear, no problem. He's so strong. A week after the Tour de France, you see him at the Clásica de San Sebastián and he's 100 per cent again. Put some guys next to him on the same training schedule, and boom, they're totally fried three weeks later. Improvements in how we understand individual bodies has closed the gap, because now we actually know what we're doing. Before it was just guess work. And it was the same with medication and doping. They had no idea what they were up to, it was just hit and miss. They used to take amphetamines, for Christ's sake, or Pot belge, a random concoction that usually involved cocaine, heroin, amphetamines, caffeine, and whatever else the soigneur had lying around. Gino Bartali smoked cigarettes because his doctor had diagnosed him with a slow heartbeat. Does erythropoietin and testosterone and all the other crazy shit that the dopers take help? Sure it does. But poor old Joe Papp, who testified in the USADA arbitration hearing about Floyd Landis's positive result for testosterone in the 2006 Tour de France, took so much EPO that he had a haematocrit of 58 per cent, so his blood must have been as thick as soup and he couldn't even get a spot on a top team, never mind win a race.

So instead of complaining about losing out on these great careers, if those guys would take an honest look at themselves in the mirror, they'd admit that there were other factors. Phil Gaimon is a case in point. He's very vocal on social media and in the press, and he's written a couple of books, all with the same underlying message: 'I was robbed.' Now he's retired, there's a bitterness and a belief that he couldn't stay in the pro peloton because the game is rigged, but in all the tweets, interviews, books, and YouTube videos he's put out, he's never once considered that maybe he just didn't have what it takes. I liked his books and he seems like a nice guy, but the whole 'woe is me' thing is infuriating. He goes around with his 'Clean' tattoo, and tries to take the quickest time records on big climbs that are held by convicted or alleged dopers, and that's the act.

In 2017 he had a cheap shot at his old teammate, the Portuguese domestique Andre Cardoso, who returned an Adverse Analytical Finding for EPO just before the Tour. Phil decided that he was the resident expert and took to Twitter to denounce Cardoso and make fun of his bland press release, which the American felt sounded like he 'didn't give a shit'. I saw that and thought, Cardoso is about to lose everything, it's right before the Tour de France and he's dragging his team through the dirt, and he probably has managers and an agent telling him he needs to get a statement out. They probably helped him, because English is going to be Cardoso's second or possibly third language, and Phil Gaimon thinks he has the right to give him a lesson on semantics? Maybe the statement lacked heart, but who cares? That's not what makes a person guilty or innocent. In 2015, Gaimon defended his friend Tom Danielson when he was accused of cheating, purely on the basis that Danielson went crazy on Twitter, pleading his innocence. Then a year later, Danielson accepted a four-year ban from the US Anti-Doping Agency after testing positive for a prohibited substance, the second time he'd been done for an anti-doping violation. I don't know why he deserved defending, just because he was a better liar, but to me that's the perfect illustration of what's wrong with a lot of cycling commentary. There are too many opinions and not enough facts, and the waters are all too often muddied further by personal relationships.

I know that a lot of my generation were pissed off because they feel like they've been robbed of jobs. They're frustrated and that gets given a lot of space in the media, even though it doesn't reflect what most of the bunch thinks. I hear a lot that Christian Vande Velde gets $200,000 a year for eighty days' work on NBC and they don't think he deserves that because he was a cheat. Maybe they're right, but at the same time, they don't deserve it just for being clean, either. Christian seems to be good at his job, he sounds nice on TV and he knows his stuff – that's what he's getting paid for. It's a new career for him, and what matters is Christian the cycling expert, not Christian the doper. They don't like that Christian has a job at NBC, because he's part of the Armstrong era. It doesn't matter that Christian is good at it, in their eyes he doesn't deserve anything because he doped back when he rode for US Postal.

I also don't understand the big deal surrounding Lance Armstrong's return to the cycling world, or about him going to the Ronde van Vlaanderen. Love or hate him, he still gets a lot of attention, and plenty of people will come to see him and hear what he has to say. You only have to look at the success of his podcasts to realise that. During the Tour de France in 2018, half of the bunch was going to bed every night listening to his daily show. He did some terrible things and he lied for a long time, but in the context of his era, I don't think he was unique in that respect.

If you want to say that Lance did a lot of damage to cycling, that's fair. But he didn't do it alone. Some people can make it seem like he was the only cyclist to ever dope, cheat, or lie. Some of the biggest legends in the sport are proven cheats and dopers though, so I think it's a bit unfair to excommunicate Armstrong with one breath and then heap praise on some old guy who just did it before they could text properly. I think you can hate the sin, without hating the sinner. Not that I want him forgiven or think he's an angel, it's just that I don't think it's helpful to anyone to keep flogging the guy for the same crime. If we were to kick everyone who's ever been involved with doping out of the sport, most of the teams would be looking for a new sports director, manager, or doctor.

Armstrong has been cast as this supervillain because he was the most forceful and aggressive when challenged, and ultimately, because he was the best at doping and more methodical than his dirty rivals. But the only one of those charges that's against the regulations is the doping. There's nothing in the UCI rulebook that says you can't be an arsehole, or that you deserve a special kind of damnation simply because you didn't get caught as quickly as the others did.

He's still in touch with some guys in the peloton, even the ones he doesn't know personally. He reaches out to people on social media, or sends them private messages when he likes what they're doing. I know a couple of guys who've gotten calls from him with advice, and they were happy to hear from him and listen to what he had to say because he's also a master of the sport. The drugs didn't help him with tactics, after all, so he knows what he's talking about when it comes to race craft. I haven't spent that much time around him, but when I had a big crash a few years ago, the first message I saw on my phone when I woke up in the hospital was from him. That's the other side of him.

In fairness to Phil Gaimon, he's honest about his own abilities. He raced until the end of 2016, and it was definitely possible to be a competitive bike rider then without dope. Judging from the watts he puts out when he publishes his climbs online, he could still be a pro if he wanted to be because he's strong, but you have to want it, and if you're only making $65,000 a year, perhaps the sacrifices just aren't worth it. Being away from home is hard, and even harder if you want to be in California but have to sit in an apartment in Girona alone for most of the year. There's a misguided belief that because some riders chose not to dope in a dirty era that they're somehow more deserving of a job after retirement. The real world doesn't work like that. If it did, there would be very few people who deserved their jobs.

As far as cycling today goes, I think a lot has changed but there is still more work to be done. I've always been two or three metres from the edge when it comes to medication, so I'm not worried about slipping, but when you're standing on the precipice, it's easy to fall off. And I fully believe that some teams are gaming the system, using every available tool to get an athlete to 100 per cent, including the abuse of TUEs and substances that aren't banned. I say abuse, because to me, that's what it is. I don't care if it's only paracetamol, if you're taking it because you think you've found some clever way to improve your performance, that's a misuse of that substance. It might not be against the letter of the law, but it's certainly against the spirit of it.

For me, TUEs should be more closely scrutinised and WADA and the UCI should be making a very public effort to punish anyone who abuses the system. And if someone goes over the limit, knowingly or by mistake, there should be consequences. It doesn't always have to be a two year ban, that would be a bit harsh when no one is sure if things like asthma drugs can actually do anything for your performance or not, but it can't just go unpunished. It sends the wrong message. Even if the rider didn't do it on purpose, if he just kept puffing on his inhaler because he was panicking and under a lot of pressure, he still went over the limit and that's against the rules. Getting a fine or a ban for a silly rush of blood to the head might suck, but this is part of the job. Knowing the rules is as much a part of being a pro athlete as training and competing. If I get sick, go to the pharmacy, buy some random selection of drugs, and take them all in the hope that I'll feel better soon – like I think almost everyone who isn't a professional cyclist does – and there's something in one of them that's banned and shows up in a doping test, that's my fault. I didn't break the rules to cheat, but I did break the rules out of laziness. I need to be 100 per cent sure of what I'm putting into my body at all times. That's a requirement of this life, the same as training and watching my diet. Ignorance isn't an excuse, any more than it would be if I got caught by the police driving twice the speed limit.

Aside from punishment, I also think that the race organisers and the UCI need to be a lot clearer about what happens in these situations. Some riders are clear to race while being investigated, some aren't. Some teams will pull you from competition, some will let you keep going.

In my opinion, it would be better if nothing is ever announced until after the B sample is examined, but it is rare. Going back to Cardoso as an example, he was suspended immediately for an Adverse Analytical Finding in June 2017, before a B sample had been tested and only days before the start of the Tour de France. Trek-Segafredo suspended him immediately and effectively ended his career. Officially, the line from WADA is that all athletes are presumed innocent until the relevant anti-doping organisation establishes an anti-doping rule violation (an ADRV in their language). Cardoso is still protesting his innocence, because testing on the B sample concluded that it was 'doubtful but inconclusive regarding the presence of recombinant EPO,' according to the UCI's own report. He was then given a four-year ban in 2018, even though according to WADA guidelines, a negative B sample should override the A sample. The UCI could do this because the findings were categorised as an 'Atypical Finding,' allowing them to interpret the results as they wished. Not that it matters, really, because at his age, once Cardoso missed out on that Tour and had his contract terminated, he'd already been given his sentence.

I can understand both sides of the argument, but we need to decide on protocol and stick to it. If a rider is innocent until proven guilty, then the results of an A sample should never be made public until the B is tested, and everyone should be allowed to continue racing until they are either cleared or found guilty. If it's more important for the sport to be seen being proactive about cheating, then the second someone returns a problematic A sample, they should be sent on gardening leave while their case is processed as quickly as possible.

This is something that doesn't only affect teams and riders. It can damage the reputation of a race, and turn a historic sporting event into a meaningless farce. For example, in 2011, when Alberto Contador was under investigation for a clenbuterol positive, he was allowed to race the Giro d'Italia. He duly won, only to have his title stripped shortly after. It made a mockery of a great event and made the whole sport look stupid.

The UCI rulebook already allows riders in a similar position to be excluded from a race, but it's open to interpretation. Rule number 2.2.010bis states that: 'The organiser may refuse permission to participate in – or exclude from – an event, a team or one of its members whose presence might be prejudicial to the image or reputation of the organiser or of the event.' I think 'may' is the important word there. It leaves the decision to the race organiser, who understandably wants the biggest stars at his race and is therefore unlikely to take responsibility for excluding them.

I also think that transparency is crucial because public pressure can be effective. If a team is constantly getting TUEs, everyone should know about it. I can think of a couple of teams who I wish would explain to the rest of the peloton how the therapeutic use exemptions that their riders keep getting before the biggest races don't affect performance. In a way, it's actually worse than the dirty years, because at least you knew what you were dealing with back then. Now, if a rider takes a banned medication with obvious performance-enhancing potential, the kind of stuff my team would never allow me to use even with a TUE, it's OK because they have a doctor's note.

If you'll excuse the pun, that's a bitter pill to swallow. I tried to be as skinny as possible for years, but it's a lot easier to shed weight when you're using cortisone. I was starving myself, only to line up at a race beside someone lighter who had just had a convenient shot of triamcinolone in his arse. That's a corticosteroid that can be used to treat allergies and skin conditions, but it also causes weight loss, improving power to weight ratio. Misusing drugs to aid weight loss is the same as abusing them to increase power or stamina, because it's having a similar effect on your performance. The public might think that doping to build muscle with steroids is more serious than taking something to lose weight, but not in the context of professional sports. Getting down to five per cent body fat is the best thing you can do if you want to win stage races. If you're down to that and then you go and dope, there will obviously be an improvement, but if you can't shed that extra mass, you'll never amount to anything. A kilo can be the difference between attacking and being dropped. So you can take all the EPO you want, but if you still weigh 85 kilograms, you're not winning anything in the mountains.

I got down to their weight by starving myself. I didn't want to be the stupid fat guy compared to them so I did everything I could, which meant that I was almost always fasting. You know that you're too skinny when it starts to affect how your body functions, but I've ridden several Grand Tours where I haven't even been able to get an erection. I'd go the last two weeks of the race without being able to get a boner. That's a crazy situation for a young guy to put himself in, but that's the truth. My testosterone level would be so low that it didn't matter what I was looking at, I didn't care. I didn't have the energy for it. You could see it in my levels on my biological passport. Around the time of a competition, most teams wouldn't allow the use of medication that can greatly aid weight loss, but some do. It all depends on which side of the ethical fence you sit. I don't understand why a sport with a troubled doping past would allow such a massive grey area.

It's the same with inhalers and asthma medication. Everyone on social media these days seems to be an expert on asthma and how it should be treated, but there are so many contradictory opinions that I don't know what to believe. Which is weird, because I use one, like lots of riders. There are dozens of guys in the bunch who have one and use it regularly, and no one ever goes over. I've been tested countless times throughout my career, and the inhaler is not something that I ever once thought would cause a problem for me. It always seemed like the limit was set so high that you just couldn't exceed it unless you were up to something dodgy. I'd take two puffs before a stage if I needed it and then just throw it into my rain bag and forget about it. It didn't occur to me to think about it at all until 2018, when it felt like most of the cycling news I read was more interested in asthma drugs than it was in racing. I looked into it and the first thing that jumped out at me was something called a 'paradoxical bronchospasm', a known side-effect of the medication that actually constricts airflow. High dosages and excessive usage could only increase the likelihood of side-effects, so I don't think any medical professional working at a team is going to advise it. Even if you're cynical about it and say that the team might not care about the rider's wellbeing, constricted airflow is going to negatively affect performance, the opposite of what they want. The rules and consequences should be clearer though. If there's a limit, it should be enforced, and anyone who goes over it should be banned, regardless of their intentions. It's the only way to protect the rest of us.

THE UCI

There's so much bullshit and politicking surrounding the UCI that, to be honest, I stopped paying attention to them a long time ago. Pat McQuaid was supposed to sort things out after Hein Verbruggen, Brian Cookson was billed as a fresh start after McQuaid, and now David Lappartient is blaming everything on his predecessors and promising that his presidency will be the one to finally turn things around. I'm not holding my breath. To borrow a phrase from Lappartient's mother tongue, *plus ça change, plus c'est la même chose.* The more things change, the more they stay the same.

Cycling has been my whole life and even I get confused about what's happening sometimes. The inauguration of the WorldTour was supposed to change everything, but I think more or less we're in the same position. A few of the biggest teams are more powerful, but the average team, the riders, and most of the races are all just as vulnerable as they've ever been. Things have improved somewhat, but the sport as a whole is nowhere near being sustainable and secure. Even changes that should be relatively easy rarely happen. They've been talking about reducing the number of riders at races since I turned pro, but they're only getting around to it now. You can't count on them to do anything.

The UCI isn't ever a topic at the dinner table when we're at the races. I'm not even sure what makes Lappartient different to Cookson because I couldn't have been bothered to read his manifesto. No one there resonates with me because they don't

seem serious about tackling the biggest problems facing professional cycling.

Financially, the sport is a basket case. There's no security
for teams or riders and very little certainty for race organisers.
Everyone involved with racing does it because they love cycling.
If they didn't, they'd do something else because there are easier
ways of making a living. That passion will always keep the
sport going, it's almost like life support in that sense, because
no matter how bad it gets there'll always be someone crazy
enough to want to race, and there'll always be someone mad
enough to invest their money to make that happen. But if we're
talking about being a major sport in the modern sense, serious
work needs to be done to attract more investment and create
more opportunities.

In terms of salary, the current minimum in the WorldTour
is probably fair, if you ask me. To recap, a neo-pro earns at
least €25,806 at Pro Continental level and €30,839 on a
WorldTour team. I don't think they need to do much with that.
It's not a lot, but for a young guy it's enough to start a career.
I don't think we need any millionaire teenagers running around,
like in football. It's a different story for the women. Most of
them have to work day jobs to survive and that's totally unjus-
tifiable. I've said elsewhere that this is professional sport and
we get paid what the market decides to pay us, but the UCI
could do a lot to give women's racing more exposure, which
in turn would make it easier to attract sponsors and raise wages.
But that's another example of things they talk about but never
do – Cookson promised to bring in a minimum wage for women
riders when he was running for election in 2013, but Lappartient
was the one to announce it and it's not coming until 2020.

The UCI needs to make sure that it's promoting the best
kind of racing possible, and that means modernising in some
areas and putting restrictions elsewhere. I'm not always the

biggest fan of Alberto Contador, but we agree on one thing. He's talked a lot about getting rid of power meters from racing and I'm with him, even though I was one of the early adopters. Especially in the time trials. It just makes it too easy for the strongest guys, because it eliminates the human element of racing. They know their limit and all they have to do is watch the little screen. The power meters have made everyone a time-trial specialist, because it takes no skill to pace yourself any more. Before, you had to go by feeling, and that was a hard thing to learn. It puts the natural TT talents at a big disadvantage, the same as it does the great climbers. Those guys can feel their limits and know when to push, and if you're trying to keep up and you just go a couple of per cent past your own limit, it can be devastating. You fall to pieces. It's what used to make racing so exciting, but you never see the best guys crack now. Not really. Someone might lose a few seconds in the last kilometres of a huge climb, but we've lost too much of the drama.

It's not about going back to the dark ages, either. Power meters are an incredible training tool, but I think they should be left at that. Other sports like Formula One and Moto GP are constantly revising what technology to allow and what to ban, because they know that they need to keep that human fallibility to ensure exciting racing. I would love to see just how good a racer Chris Froome really is, for example. On a purely physical level, he might be the best of his generation, but I'm not sure I'd be betting on him without the power meter and his race radio. Even when he has a mechanical or he's not feeling great, he's able to make a quick calculation and just stare at his output to pace himself to the finish.

Look at the Hour Record. On paper, it's just a guy going around in circles, but what makes it fascinating is the fact that he's alone against the clock. When I was growing up I remember they banned the use of lights that some people wanted to shine just ahead of the rider to pace him around the velodrome, and for me, the power meter is pretty much the same thing. You can do your testing, someone sets a level for you to maintain, and then you just follow your little computer from the start until the finish. Everyone's output is unique, but if someone attacks me on a climb now, I can estimate how long he'll be able to maintain that effort based on my own readings. If I didn't have a power meter to look at, I'd have to make a call based on my gut. That would make the racing more unpredictable and also favour the more speculative, exciting riders. It might be safer for everyone too because I know of a few people in the bunch who spend most of the day staring at their computer rather than the road ahead.

Other than ensuring that the racing is as good as it can be, I think the UCI needs to do much more on safety. Just as one example, they limit how light a bike frame can be and all the manufacturers need to conform to UCI standards, but what about other equipment? I can remember a few cases of exploding wheels in the last year or two, and I'm not convinced that the powers that be are doing enough to check that everyone's gear is safe to race with. My team has good sponsors and I'm certain that it's all bombproof, but that's no good to me if someone else is using some poorly made carbon wheel that crumbles and causes him to hit the deck right in front of me when we're travelling at speed.

The decision to cut team sizes will have a big impact, and not just on the style of racing. Up until 2017, we had nine riders at the Grand Tours and seven at the others, but now the teams are only sending eight guys to the Giro d'Italia, the Tour de France, and the Vuelta a España. Personally, that makes life more difficult because it's going to be hard for everyone to justify their inclusion. I can see how this move might make things more interesting for the neutrals, people who aren't directly involved in racing such as fans and journalists, but for the riders, it's shit. Teams will be smaller and there's more competition for fewer places. Even the biggest teams can afford to cut people now because they don't need as many riders to cover a whole WorldTour season.

It probably won't get noticed away from the peloton and none of the redundancies are going to make headlines, because they're the guys at the bottom of the roster. That makes it less relevant for the fans and less likely to make the news, but it doesn't make it any easier on a hard-working pro who has suddenly found himself unemployed. As just one example, Movistar went from a twenty-eight-man roster in 2017 to 25 in 2018 and BMC went from twenty-nine to twenty-four. If you take three or four riders from each of the eighteen WorldTour teams, that's a lot of guys out of work. Most of them will be able to drop down to Continental level, but there's an obvious knock-on effect there and whatever way you look at it, it means fewer professional cyclists. Maybe that's a good thing – I just don't think it was given enough consideration. Perhaps it wouldn't be so difficult to swallow if there were more opportunities for those riders to race elsewhere on the calendar. I can understand the motivation behind it, and I hope it makes for more exciting racing.

I think it will be interesting to see how it plays out in the Grand Tours over the next couple of seasons, because I don't think most teams will be strong enough to fight on more than one front any more. They'll have to decide if they want to go for the general classification, or if they want to back a sprinter or someone who will hunt for stages in the mountains. I can't see a way to build a team that can protect a GC guy and still provide a good lead-out train for the sprints. It was hard enough for Team Sky to do it back in 2012 when they tried to support

Brad Wiggins and Mark Cavendish, and in the end, it was Cav who suffered, so I don't think anyone will be doing it effectively with eight riders.

From the sponsors' perspective, it's a different thing altogether. With fewer riders to pay, teams are going to be less expensive. If that makes funding a team more attractive and the financial side of the sport becomes more dependable, then it will be worth it. An optimist would look at it and hope that it will make teams more financially sound, and by improving the racing, it will also make the sport more appealing, which in turn will bring in more money. A pessimist would say that teams used to have ten riders at the Giro and the Tour back in the 1980s and reducing the size to nine did little or nothing to stabilise the sport, make it safer, or grow the sport. And Lappartient is already talking about reducing team sizes further, so there could be more lay-offs in the near future. I think a smaller peloton will make for more exciting racing, and in theory, it might help to reduce the number of crashes as well. But I don't think cutting numbers is a panacea that can solve all cycling's problems.

BEING MARRIED TO A PROFESSIONAL CYCLIST

It would be impossible to have a long cycling career without the support of your family, so when I started this book I knew that my wife deserved her say, too. So here she is, in her own words.

When we chose our home, it was all about balance. He needs to train and for that he needs to be near good roads and decent cycling terrain, but with all of the training camps they do these days, we didn't have to make a huge sacrifice and move somewhere just for the cycling because there's a lot more to our lives. The most important thing is to put the hours in, it's not like he needs to be climbing big mountains every day. I can see why some other riders are attracted to living in places like Lugano in Switzerland or Monte Carlo in Monaco, but that wasn't for us. I wanted to be somewhere that was good for kids and where I felt comfortable, where I could have friends and my own life, because he's away for so much of the year.

As we got older and our priorities changed, it was important to be relatively close to family too. When we lived abroad they'd visit, but it was just for the weekend and it was always complicated, so it's nice to be able to see them more often and call them when I need a hand.

Like every relationship, there are always two sides to a story, and what works for one might not work for the other. Other places we've lived, I found the people to be a little cold or unfriendly, whereas he thought they were all great. I'd have to remind him that they were only smiling and being chatty because he was famous, it wasn't like that for me. I remember going shopping with him once and he was talking about how much he liked it, how neighbourly everyone was, offering him a coffee or whatever, and I had to remind him, 'Hey, you're a professional athlete! That's why they want to talk to you.' No one was offering me anything! He laughed, and admitted I might have had a point. When you're famous, your view is always a bit blurred by the celebrity, it becomes normal to get the best table in a restaurant without making a booking, or for the guy in the market to call you by your name and skip you to the front of the queue.

The first place we lived, we were there for a couple of years and we hardly knew anyone. We made some friends, of course, and there were other riders there so it wasn't all bad, but we didn't know anyone on our street, no one ever said hi. I used to think, jokingly, 'Is it something we said?' He's on the road for weeks at a time, so I'm the one who actually has to live in a place full-time, and finding the right balance between his professional needs and the family's needs was crucial. I also have my own career to think about, so it's not like I just want to sit around in cafes or on a beach somewhere, either.

When we were younger, it was more attractive to travel and to try new places, but when you've been doing it a while, the allure wears off. It's harder, physically and mentally, to be away from everyone all the time. And not just for me, I don't think it's in his best interests either. He misses home when he's away, more than he used to, and I know he loves being here with me and the kids, and with our friends as well. He wants to be here to play with the kids or read stories. It's nice to come back to reality, because professional cycling can be a bit of a bubble.

Having a family has to put some things in perspective, too. He's as committed as ever in terms of training and enthusiasm for racing, but I don't think he's taking as many risks as he might have ten years ago. I hope not, anyway. Racing bikes is always dangerous, but it doesn't have to be pure insanity. It's not worth risking your life for a couple of seconds. Age makes you realise that. It used to be more important for him to be at the front all of the time, even when he didn't need to be, because he didn't want to miss out on the action. He manages himself much better now, which is funny in a way, because that maturity is giving him more energy, which has prolonged his career at an age when most riders would be retired. He used to be so wasted all the time. He's not like that any more. He'd come home totally screwed, with no energy for anything, and for a few days it was like he was down some dark hole. Now he comes home from a Grand Tour and right away, he's talking about taking the kids out to play, or about where we'll all go for a nice lunch. It's great. That's my husband coming back, not some maniac who only thinks about fitness and racing form.

Of course, that attitude is only possible because he's one of the senior riders on the team now, and they want him as much for his knowledge and experience as they do his legs. It wasn't like that five or six years ago, when he was competing at the very top. Back then, the salary was a lot higher, but so were the demands and the pressures. So you have to take the good with the bad. I'm happy for him that he's been able to experience different roles in the peloton, and I think this is a great way to transition into the next phase of his life. Going cold turkey is too hard, there are too many changes.

Before a Grand Tour, he'll get more prickly as the race gets closer. He's more agitated, and you can feel his competitive nature coming to the fore. He'll need to win every discussion, even when it's got nothing to do with cycling, even if it's just something silly. He'll come in right away with his opinion, which is always the right opinion, of course. And I'll be left thinking, 'Really?' It makes sense, of course. He needs that competitive edge, he wouldn't be much of a bike racer if he didn't want to win. We like to joke about it. I'll tell him, 'Oh, you must be in really good shape now, because you're turning into a bit of an arsehole!' And we'll laugh.

Sleeping becomes more difficult; with more training he becomes far more sensitive to sounds and light. That's easy for me to understand and I always try to work around it, but it must be hard for the kids because it's not so easy to explain why someone's mood changes like that. It's not like he means to be like that, obviously, but with the stress of training and the mental pressure leading up to a bike race, it's only natural that someone's temperament is going to change. You can see it when he talks to strangers too. He's just not interested, he's off in his own world, he won't make eye contact, he'll just look at the ground and rub his face or something. It's funny to think about what kind of impression he'd make if you just met him like that, a week before the Giro or the Tour, because he's normally a friendly, good-humoured guy.

I don't even think the most taxing part of that for him is the physical exhaustion. He loves riding his bike and he manages his body well. I think it's the mental fatigue of it all, because when he's not riding his bike, there's always someone looking for him. It could be a sponsor, or the media, charity events, business engagements … even his friends. He's not around very often, so they're all happy to see him when he's home, even though sometimes all he really wants is some space.

I think that's the thing with professional cycling – you can't understand how much that stuff affects someone unless you're inside of it. The great thing about cycling is that anyone can go ride in the Alps or the Dolomites and experience a little bit of the excitement from all the races, but for everyone else, it's a leisure activity, you do it with your friends in your time off and you do it to enjoy it. You don't need to do all the team meetings, the press conferences, the anti-doping, the long transfers to and from the stage, the uploading of all your files to the team's database. Just being good on a bike isn't enough, you can't be a professional cyclist unless you can handle all the shit on the side. It's not something that anyone likes, but it's a huge part of being a bike racer at the top level. You have to handle all that peripheral stuff, even though none of it really has anything to do with what you signed up for as a kid.

At a race one year, I remember someone else's partner saying to me, 'I used to think it was just him.' She was relieved to see that everyone changed around a big race. The truth is that everyone involved in cycling, from the mechanics and soigneurs to the journalists and the race organisers, feel the pressure. No one suffers like the riders, of course, but regardless of what your job is, being dragged around Italy or France for three weeks, in close quarters with your colleagues and with little sleep, isn't exactly conducive to sociability. If you're at the Tour or the Giro, you'll meet someone who you know is really nice, and they'll be totally different. It could be a reporter that you've known for years, someone who'd normally be happy to come over and say hi or have a chat, but at a Grand Tour they're just balls of stress, always worrying about work, and about what still needs to be done. Welcome to the world of cycling.

At the height of his career, I think he was away for 280 days one year. It's crazy. It's exciting too, when you're young, but it's an enormous amount of pressure to put on someone, which is probably why so few riders have long, happy careers. If you think about that year, he only had those eighty-five days, spread out over the year in little parcels, to fit in everything that most people take for granted, like time with your partner or your kids, hanging out with friends and family. And it goes without saying that they weren't even proper days off, because he was still training and required to do all the secondary stuff, like team admin and media. I'm not sure if hard is the right word to use because it goes with the territory and we weren't complaining – it was his dream, after all – but it took a toll. It's hard for the guys because they're away all the time when they want to be home, and it's hard for their partners because they're trying to manage everything, probably balancing their own careers while starting a family. That was when we knew that home had to be somewhere we both loved, with friends and family nearby, and not just an apartment someplace that was good for training or tax breaks.

The other houses we had, we didn't treat them like home. If something broke, we fixed it, but we knew it wasn't where we'd be in the long run, so we didn't care about it that much. They were just places that facilitated his cycling career. But it's funny, because we found this place that we both love, and having a proper home away from the peloton is now extending that career. To a lot of other riders, I'm sure that's counter-intuitive, but there's no way he'd still be racing if we were living in a rented apartment somewhere really far from everyone we love. It felt like life was on hold in those places, his career was going great but everything else was on the back burner. We wouldn't have wanted our kids to be dragged about, because it's not fair on them, they deserve to settle in school, make friends, have a normal childhood. And it's not like it's the 1950s either, I have my own life to get on with. I don't regret what we did when we were younger, it was exciting for both of us and it's still incredible to think of everything he's achieved, but life can't be like that forever.

Aside from the itinerant lifestyle, the big downside to someone you love racing bikes for a living is obviously the crashing. Crashing is part of the job, unfortunately. I can't say it makes me happy to admit that, but it's a fact of life when you're a pro cyclist. I don't like seeing it, and most of the time I won't watch the downhill parts of races because it's too stressful. I'll calculate how long it's going to take to get into the valley or to the next climb, and I'll change channel or go do something else. When I was younger, it was only him that I worried about so I could watch a race if he wasn't in it, but now I feel for them all so I just don't watch any descents. I can't help thinking about all of the people like me watching at home. Listening to him, I know he takes care of himself and he knows what he's doing. I know that the younger guys are always happy for his advice, and he's always pointing out to me who the bad descenders are, the guys he stays well away from.

He's been lucky though, there have been some bad injuries over the years that I know were really painful and difficult for him to recover from, but compared to some guys ... But it's also true that some riders get a reputation for crashing when actually they're not that bad. I can think of a couple of his friends in the bunch who just always seem to be in front of a camera when something goes wrong, so they'll get a reputation, but then you talk to them and find out that they've never even broken a collarbone – something that even a lot of amateur riders break.

The surface wounds, ripped-up jerseys and lots of road rash, look really bad on television, but it's superficial. Once I see him riding to the finish line, I know he's not too bad. Sometimes you'll see a guy with cuts all up his back or on his face, and it looks horrific, but if the same thing happened to their leg they'd just put a bandage on it and forget about it.

Probably the biggest fear is an accident with a car when he's out training, but that's a reality for us all, not just professional riders. I'm not an expert on cycling history, but I know that a car crash almost ended Marco Pantani's career, and Bradley Wiggins was hit by a van the year he won the Tour de France. And more recently, there was that incident when a bunch of guys from the same team got run over by someone in Spain, and the case of poor Michele Scarponi, who lost his life while out training close to his home. With all the risks they take racing, it's incredible to think that the most dangerous part of the job might be riding your bike down a public road. All that said, I am thankful that we haven't had to spend too much time in hospitals over the years.

One of the biggest differences I've noticed between pro riders and 'civilians' is just how stubborn their positive attitude can be. When they crash, straight away they start thinking about recovery. 'How long is this going to take me? What can I do to come back strong?' Internally, I'm sure there's some self-pity or some doubts, but the outward attitude is one of confidence and positivity. I don't know how they can crash, break bones, lose skin, come close to a really serious injury, and still keep going like nothing ever happened. You have to be a special kind of person, maybe a little bit crazy. He says it helps to have a short memory. I just think they love cycling too much to let anything stop them.

We met when we were still pretty much kids. I knew a little bit about cycling, my dad watched the big races, but the normal stuff, what anyone who liked sport in general would know. I didn't follow it, so I could have only named the top few guys. I actually used to think it was boring, because my dad used to fall asleep sometimes during the Tour. But now when we're watching races at home, even my husband falls asleep, so I guess that's just part of cycling when you're relaxing on the couch! I love seeing the crowds, all the signs they make, and the big displays that the farmers make in their fields, there's something very old-fashioned about it that makes me smile.

We'd actually been in the same class for years before we really talked. We were out with a big group of friends to see a game. He sat next to me, and I thought, 'Hey, he might actually be interesting.' I don't think either of us had thought about it before. So it wasn't love at first sight, because we'd been around each other the whole time.

It had been a few months of dating before I realised that he had this huge opportunity. I knew he loved cycling, but I wasn't sure how good he was until he phoned me from an important race for up-and-coming amateurs, where he'd made the podium. I had no real idea what that meant – I knew that a podium was a big deal, but that was it. I didn't know that in cycling, a podium at a race like that can launch a career. I just told him: 'Good for you! That's fun.' I was thinking about my own stuff at the time, I was busy with university, and the idea of him becoming a professional still seemed like a long shot. As time passed though, the good results kept coming and his training got really serious, and it was obvious that he was made for it.

If he hadn't made it as a cyclist, it would have been fine too. He's bright and a quick learner, and now he enjoys studying. Life would have been more normal, there'd be less Lycra, for sure, but he would have had a good career doing something else. Even now when he does media work, it seems to come so naturally to him, he's an easy talker and he has good ideas. We wouldn't have worked out otherwise. I could never have been with a jock. Some of the guys you meet are just so one-dimensional, I don't know how anyone deals with them. They don't read or watch the news, they have no other interests away from cycling.

The fact that he's not like that means that he's actually excited about what he's going to do after he retires. Hopefully, he has a few more great seasons left in him, but when it's over he'll be happy with his lot and enthusiastic about his future. If cycling was all that he had, I don't know how we'd deal with it. You see it all the time when people retire like that, it's this huge loss, like a death in the family. They're scared shitless, as if they're facing this black hole. He knows he can do more than just ride a bike, and even though it's fair to say that he's old for a professional athlete, he's still a young man in the grand scheme of things. Cycling is a huge part of his life, but it's not the whole thing. He's always reading – magazines, one or two newspapers a day, he has piles of books – and I know he's looking forward to using his intelligence to do something else when cycling is done.

His friends in and out of the sport are similar to him and I'm happy for that because we can talk about other things. I like bikes, but it's not what I want to talk about when I'm at a party or out for a drink. The WAGs are even worse – they're just the wife of an athlete and nothing else. No thanks.

We actually laugh about that too, because we never talk about racing when he calls me. Some of his roommates over the years would phone home and then rattle on about watts and who followed whose wheel. We never did that. If he wants to have those talks, he can do it with someone from the team, because it doesn't really interest me. I understand that technical side of it, but it's not compelling to me, if we're talking about the race I want to know about the places he saw, maybe some-where where we should go back to on holiday, or if he had fun, how he was feeling. Most of the time we talk about my day and what's going on at home, because when you boil it down, his day was just 250 kilometres of cycling hard, it's the same thing he does all the time. There are more interesting things happening around here.

I've not gone to a lot of his races. When we were younger it seemed like more fun, but I preferred the ones that were closer to home because the travel made things too complicated. And when he's racing, he's in that zone, it's a totally different head space, so I'd be on my own or with the other girlfriends. I liked the national championships, so I always went to those, and his first Grand Tour, that was a special occasion. I went with a friend and we made a big deal of it, driving into the mountains for a really big stage to cheer him on. Then we saw him on the rest day, and went home. It was a great experience, and to see someone you love reach the highest level like that was amazing, but I never wanted to follow him around the whole time. Partly that's because I'd be bored, and partly it's because I knew it would have been a huge burden to him, knowing I was there, feeling obliged to meet me whenever he had a moment for a coffee or a chat. Even on the rest days, it's hard to find a few minutes to see someone because of all the media obligations and the team stuff. When he's at the races, his days are full enough already. He doesn't need any extra distractions. I went to the Champs-Élysées a few times, and that used to be fun. In the earlier years of his career the teams would spend more money for big parties and dinners, but now it's become far more serious and they're a lot more careful with their money. I heard from a few people that some teams even charge the riders if their partners come to stay.

Anyway, if it's a big race I can see it better on television and I don't have to drop everything to fly around the world after him. That's good for him too, I hope, because it helps to keep him grounded and remind him that there's more to the world than professional cycling. I have my own life to lead. That's not meant to be uncaring or dismissive, I admire everything he's done and I love the fact that he followed his dream and achieved some special things, but at the end of the day, I'm his wife, not a fan.

RETIREMENT

It might sound counter-intuitive, but it's actually physically easier for me to race a Grand Tour now than it was when I was younger because I'm not chasing my own general classification goal. When you're trying to win a Grand Tour or make the top five or top ten, it never lets up, you have to give absolutely every last drop of energy that you can find until the line, no matter what's happened. It's different when you're working as a domestique or a road captain for someone else. I still have my job to do, but when the GC guys start trading blows on the final kilometres of the last climb, I don't have to struggle to hang on to them like I would have when I was younger. It's OK for me to be dropped now and ride in at my own pace, in between the leaders and the gruppetto behind. You'll see some riders racing for twenty-fifth place on a stage, but I couldn't care less about that. I've been at the top, so to me there's no satisfaction in sprinting with someone just to finish twenty-ninth instead of thirtieth.

Based on my training data and the values that the team tracks, and on how I feel generally, I'm sure I still have the ability to race for a top-fifteen or top-twenty placing at a Grand Tour, but it doesn't interest me. I'd rather work as part of a team for a bigger goal, and share what I've learned with my younger teammates. The only effect of ageing that I notice for sure is that it takes longer to heal when things go wrong, so taking really good care of yourself is essential if you want to have a long career. I had a bad injury a few years back that took ages to recover fully from, but eventually I got over it and

I feel better now than I did then. I was worried that I was going to be that way for ever, like an old man with all these aches and pains, so now that the problem has been fixed I feel young again. Or young enough, anyway. My knees hurt when I'm playing with the kids and I wonder is that from cycling, but I don't know how other dads in their thirties feel. Maybe they're fucked too.

Once they have the right mindset, older riders are valuable to a team because we're focused on doing our jobs. I want to help the leaders win races now and pass on my knowledge, the days of dreaming about my own victories are over. I'm still good enough to win some smaller races, but after everything I've done in my career, that doesn't interest me. I want to be at the biggest races, and if you look at the stage winners at the Giro or the Tour these days, they're all top riders. The days of the speculative breakaway winner seem to be over. Or it's a lot rarer than it used to be, at least. With the younger riders in the team, there's more ego and more expectation, the bosses have to keep giving them little bones to chase because otherwise they might not follow the script when it really matters. You can't afford to have someone thinking of themselves when you're going for a major goal like a Classic or a Grand Tour. It's only one guy on the podium, but it's the whole team that puts him there.

It's nice to be able to enjoy it while it lasts. I want to be racing for another couple of years, but you never know. One bad injury and it could be over. So I'm always trying to soak it all up and savour the moment. You'll see a lot of young guys get down when things don't go their way, but I'm always telling them, 'Cheer up, you can't let a fall or a runny nose ruin this for you, you're living your dream.' If they want to do it for ten or fifteen years, they need to have a positive mentality about it all, even when it sucks. If a cold is going to make you depressed, it's going to be a tough career, because you're going to get a few of them every season, no matter what. And if they're pissed off because they couldn't finish a race, I just tell them to train better next time. You have to keep your eyes forward, there's no point dwelling on what's already happened.

It makes me laugh when I see a rider who's just retired talking about how much he enjoys cycling again, boasting about not having to use a power meter any more. What are they talking about? Are they actually saying that they didn't enjoy riding while they were pro? That's too depressing to think about, because all you do is ride when you're a pro. If you don't like the power meter, don't use it. I know lots of riders who just train on feel, sprint when they want to, get out of the saddle when they feel good, or race their friends to the stop sign. You're still riding really hard, it just seems like more fun. No one is forcing you to train with a power meter – it just makes it easier for some people. It's not like there's some law forcing you to stare at that screen all day. The important thing is that you show up for training camps and races in great shape.

On the whole, the bike keeps you young. I've gotten some of my old schoolfriends back into riding and we'll do some stuff on the weekend or go mountain biking at night after work, and they love it, because it's like playing again. And personally, it helps that I'm not thinking about a definitive retirement date any more. I used to, but now I'm trying to go with the flow and just enjoy it. The team is thinking like that too. Before too long they won't need my legs, but my brain can still be useful, coaching the younger guys, organising things like training camps, or perhaps in corporate, because I like talking to people and (I think) that they like me. I'd love to be given the freedom to organise a cool training camp, not in some shitty hotel in Spain, but somewhere special where there was more to do than just ride, eat, and sleep, maybe allowing some time for some mountain biking too. You train just as hard that way, but you have fun, and for me at least, that makes it seem easier. The more I study, the more I think I'm suited to the preparation side of the team. I love the tactics during the race, but I don't know if I want to be in a team car as a director for seven hours every day during a Grand Tour.

My ultimate dream would be to have my own team, something small to start with. I still have a lot to learn though. After so many years, I have some clue, but I don't know the intricate details. It's like being a waiter at a Michelin-starred restaurant for ten years; you'll understand a lot of things, but that doesn't make you a chef. I need to have a good look in the kitchen and see how the whole thing is made.

It's also hard to see it from the management's point of view when you're still a rider. I know we moan about some things that probably seem silly to them, and I know we do some things that come across as totally braindead. It's common for guys to put a photo on social media that will really upset a sponsor, for instance, because he's there in a different brand of sunglasses or in a jersey that doesn't have their logo on it, and they've paid a lot of money for that. That's how this sport works, but we'll forget, and it never seems like that big of a deal. I used to think they were just being dickheads about it, but as I've gotten older I see the importance of it. Once I got an angry lecture from the team manager because there was a photo of me on Instagram out mountain biking, and I wasn't in team kit. I didn't see the big deal, because everything I was using had come from the equipment sponsor, just from their MTB line. I pointed that out to the boss, and he went crazy, shouting, 'Of course *they're* happy with you, you're advertising all their stuff. But what about the other sponsors? They want their logos on there too.' He was right, of course. It doesn't seem important to me as a rider, but I'd be pissed if I gave a team a big cheque and then I saw one of their guys putting photos up in front of hundreds of thousands of followers without my company's branding.

I liked my first team because it was so small, I always worked with the same DS. Now, there are directors on the team that I see once a year. I'd like to build something from a small base and see where it goes. That first DS never had to call us to see how we were feeling, for example, because he knew from being with us all the time. It's easier to manage that way, but that kind of model has limits.

The DS function in a big team is totally different; it's more about tactics and logistics, who goes where, who gets bottles on which mountain. He doesn't ask about diet because the team has dietitians, and he doesn't ask about training because all the riders are working with separate coaches. And he has to write reports all the time. There's a lot of paperwork because the organisation has gotten so big. Some teams will have a development team and a women's team too, so that could be upwards of sixty riders, with all the staff that comes with a group that big. At a small team, the DS has to do all of that. He's managing all the aspects of a rider's day-to-day life. My first DS never had to write a report in his life because there was no one to read it afterwards but him.

My team would be twelve to sixteen riders, preferably one programme, with me as manager and then one DS. Something like Axel Merckx's team, Hagens Berman Axeon, they do a great job. I'm also wondering more and more about the future of cycling, the older I get, because I see a big change coming. The surge in popularity has been a surprise to me, but gravel riding is getting really big, so perhaps some teams could target that scene and build from there. Reaching the top of road racing would be really hard, even getting anywhere near the big races would require a lot of luck and plenty of money. Even Wanty–Groupe Gobert, the small Belgian team that made their debut at the Tour de France in 2017 thanks to a wildcard invitation, has a budget of around €4 million. That's not a lot in the context of professional sports these days, but it's not something that you can do on your own or pay for out of your own pocket.

You've got to convince sponsors to trust you with considerable amounts of investment and that's no easy feat in cycling, where there are so many experienced and successful team managers struggling to put together budgets. That said, I think a lot of teams are pretty bad at monetising their brands and attracting new investment. Most of them go the same route, a big businessman that they know loves cycling and is willing to pump his own money into a team as a hobby or a vanity project. You don't see too many teams really try to market themselves and most of them are terrible with social media. They want the new money, but they're still old-fashioned and unwilling to change. Some riders are coming up with really innovative ways to make extra cash for themselves, with public events, their own merchandise, limited-edition products with their own sponsors like Oakley. I know guys that are selling more T-shirts and things like that on their own personal sites than their teams manage, because the official team site might just have a cycling kit and some bottles on a basic web shop, or maybe there'll be no shop at all. They don't bother to push the new season kits or really promote their sponsors in any meaningful way. I think the media does more for the bike companies than the teams, for example. A lot of managers just want to get the contracts, make sure they have all the bikes, clothing, and everything else that they need, and then not think about it. The old-school guys might say that winning races is the best kind of publicity for them, but you can promote sponsors in other ways and I think if teams were more proactive and inventive, they'd have less trouble. It's something I'll be paying close attention to within my own team in the coming year or two because they're one of the better ones when it comes to innovation and careful financial planning, and I have a feeling that the commercial side of running a team and the stresses that it can create is something that a lot of people underestimate when they're starting out with teams of their own.

Luckily for my personal finances, I've had good advice over the years and I started a pension at the beginning that will pay me a decent salary when I retire. That should cover me for ten years or so, which is plenty of time to figure out what I want to do. I have some property too. It's mainly just common sense, I was careful to take care of myself and my family after cycling, and you won't see me blowing huge amounts of cash on clothes or driving around in a Ferrari. I see some guys from the bunch doing really well for themselves when they retire and that gets me excited about the possibilities, too, like Christian Meier, who used to ride for Orica-GreenEdge. He lived in Girona while he was racing and chose to stay there afterwards, setting up a couple of high-end coffee shops that have since developed a reputation for being among the best in Europe. Things like that remind me that you don't have to reinvent the wheel to be successful after retirement, you just need an idea that you're passionate about.

Finding something you love, that gets you out of bed, and demands the energy and drive that you used to put into training and racing seems fundamental to a happy retirement. Otherwise, cycling is going to leave a massive void. Some guys end up drinking too much, and a lot of people get divorced. I guess it's a huge transformation for any marriage to undergo, when both of you have been used to so much time away from one another and so much structure. All of a sudden, you're at home all the time, with nothing to do.

That's probably annoying enough for most partners, especially if they're getting up and going to work every day, but more than that, it can be a huge challenge for the riders to realise that their position in the world totally changes the minute they stop racing. They're not the centre of the universe any more, and they can no longer expect friends and family to do everything just to suit them. Things like going back to university part-time, or doing media work, will help because you're surrounded by people who have their own things to worry about, it's outside of the bubble that most riders live in with their teams and their families. The journalists you'll work with and the other students in the class will know who you are, of course, but they probably don't care. And they won't give a shit about the fact that you're really tired from a big training block.

I don't think I'm egocentric compared to a lot of other professional athletes, but more and more I'm realising that I'm still a bit too selfish for the real world. I'm also sure that there'll be a steep learning curve for me to deal with when I stop racing because there's no way people are as nice to everyone as they are when they recognise me. There's a farmers' market near my old house that I used to stop in all the time on my way home from training because it had a great fishmonger and the freshest vegetables, and I was constantly telling my wife how nice everyone was. Then she went one day and came back in a bad mood. She said: 'You think they're nice? They're a bunch of ignorant dickheads.' It turns out that they'd been rude to her because she wasn't a local. They'd heard her accent, and pretended not to notice her, serving everyone else first. They were always smiling and helpful with me, but only because they'd seen me on TV. It will be weird to wait in the queue with everyone else.

It's probably easy for that to go to your head if the people around you don't keep you grounded. They say that Mario Cipollini never took a wallet with him to a restaurant, for example, because he knew that someone would buy him dinner. It was an honour for them to have him around and he knew it. He also had to have a fresh jar of jam for himself every morning at the races and training camps, so every morning a soigneur would be sure to lay one out, just so Cipo could get that satisfying pop from the lid when he opened it. Fabian Cancellara is another one with special breakfast requests. I guess he really liked papaya, because someone had to prepare it for him every morning and no one else was allowed to eat it. From what I heard, everyone knew this, apart from Bauke Mollema, who had just joined the Trek team. I know Bauke from the bunch and he's a really nice guy, very chilled out, so it wouldn't have occurred to him that this plate of fruit was a VIP thing. He ate it, no doubt delighted with himself for finding something so nice at the breakfast buffet, while all the team staff looked on, terrified to think about how Cancellara was going to react to finding half of his precious papaya missing. People will put up with that kind of silly demand when you're the main man at a team, winning Monuments or multiple stages every year at the Giro d'Italia, but away from cycling that attitude will just make you look like an oddball.

Sometimes, the thought of retirement scares me, but that's not why I'm still racing. If I allow my mind to wander, leaving this world can seem a bit daunting, but I'm here because I love it and I want to continue as long as I'm useful, but at this high level. When it's time to stop, I'll be the first to admit it. I'd love to get a sponsor who'd support me travelling the world to races like the Leadville 100 or the Cape Epic in South Africa, so that I could try some mountain-bike racing while I still have this level of fitness. It's not something that you can sustain for ten years after you retire, but for a year or two it'd be fun. Assuming, of course, that myself and my agent can find a few brands who are willing to fund the whole thing because it's not like I can dip into my savings and spend €80,000 travelling the world when I've got a wife and kids at home.

In the long run, I'm looking forward to taking it easy. I'd like to stay fit enough that if I got a call every now and then from a pro who's still riding, I could meet them for a spin and be able to keep up for a few hours. Your skill doesn't disappear, so even if your fitness drops you can hang on to someone's wheel pretty easily when they're training. You see a lot of old ex-pros like that; they look fat, but they're still dropping most amateurs on the climbs because they know their bodies better and can manage the effort. I'll keep riding, but not like this, training for six hours and then being like a zombie for the rest of the day. If I can train for a few hours in the morning and then come home to my couch, with a fire in the winter, and drink a beer in front of the television, I'll be happy. Bike-packing is awesome too, and I look forward to just riding around with my kids like a normal dad. But none of it compares to being in the Tour de France. All of those things will be waiting for me when I retire, but I'll never get another chance to do a Grand Tour. If you ever have a shot at one of those, it's not an opportunity that you can ever ignore.